"*Your Life, Your Way* takes a scientific model and makes it tangible and practical. Parents ought to buy this book for their teens. But, please parents, read it and try the exercises first. You might just change with your teens. Also, as a supervisor, I would certainly offer this book to trainees as a treatment outline. The structure is simple, direct, and flexible enough to fit real-world therapy."

—**Kelly Wilson, PhD**, professor emeritus at the University of Mississippi, founding president of the Association for Contextual Behavioral Science (ACBS), and coauthor of *Acceptance and Commitment Therapy*

"The DNA-V model is a game changer; one of the most exciting third-wave interventions in years. This cool-looking book presents the model in a way that teens will love and find helpful."

—**Ben Sedley, PhD**, clinical psychologist, and author of *Stuff That Sucks*

"Your Life, Your Way speaks authentically to young people setting out to figure out who and how they want to be. The authors' DNA-V model is a practical, accessible framework that is clearly grounded in well-researched principles of behavior change, as well as adolescent development. With meaningful questions to ponder and exercises to build new skills, this book provides exceptional tools to guide teens throughout their life's journey."

—**Siri Ming, PhD, BCBA-D**, behavior analyst, and coauthor of *Using RFT to Promote Generative Language*

"A unique, skillfully crafted tool kit for empowering young people, no matter what they are struggling with. This beautifully illustrated workbook shows young people that *they* are the person they have been waiting for—they have the power to transform and move their lives in a direction that sets their hearts on fire. I cannot think of a more perfect and timely resource for teens (and the adults who support them)."

—**Evelyn Gould, PhD, BCBA-D**, clinical behavior analyst at the New England Center for OCD and Anxiety, and research associate at Harvard Medical School

"Adolescence is a time of discovery, of taking mindful risks, and of learning flexibility in the face of the uncertainty and adversity involved in growing up in our world as it is today. This book is a gift to adolescents and their parents, as well as clinicians, teachers, counselors, and coaches who work with them. Created by Joe Ciarrochi and Louise Hayes, this brilliant book based in acceptance and commitment therapy (ACT) is just what every teen needs: a pragmatic, accessible, down-to-earth guide that will empower them to go out and live their way into their best lives. Sixteen-year-old me really, really loves this book, and highly recommends it!"

—**Lisa W. Coyne, PhD**, assistant professor in the department of psychiatry at Harvard Medical School; founder of the New England Center for OCD and Anxiety in Boston, MA; and author of *Acceptance and Commitment Therapy*

"*Your Life, Your Way* is not only filled with thoughtful and valuable guidance, it is also filled with rich, textured, and fun images and exercises. It is the perfect book to aid teenagers in relating to their emotions in an effective fashion. It is ideal for helping them build resiliency. I was wonderfully captured by each page. Ciarrochi and Hayes have 'nailed it' with this amazing self-help guide for those who are young and struggling. I might even suggest that us grown-ups could use it too! Thank you for creating such an amazing journey; it will be invaluable to all who explore its pages."

—**Robyn D. Walser, PhD**, codirector of the Bay Area Trauma Recovery Clinic; assistant professor at the University of California, Berkeley; author of *The Heart of ACT*; and coauthor of *Learning ACT* and *The Mindful Couple*

"What would it be like to own your own life? I don't mean a life that's perfect, or smooth, or easy. I mean a life that's about what your heart yearns for it to be about. That can happen, and this book is about how to get it to happen. It's based on scores of studies about people just like you, but it is easy to read, clear, and wise. If you want your life, your way—this book will show you how."

—**Steven C. Hayes, PhD**, Nevada Foundation Professor in the department of psychology at the University of Nevada, Reno; and codeveloper of ACT

JOSEPH V. CIARROCHI
& LOUISE L. HAYES

YOUR LIFE YOUR WAY

SKILLS TO HELP TEENS MANAGE EMOTIONS AND BUILD RESILIENCE

ILLUSTRATED BY KATHARINE HALL

This book belongs to:

_____

Instant Help Books

An Imprint of New Harbinger Publications, Inc.

Distributed in Canada by Raincoast Books

Copyright © 2020 by Joseph V. Ciarrochi and Louise L. Hayes
        Instant Help
        An imprint of New Harbinger Publications, Inc.
        5674 Shattuck Avenue
        Oakland, CA 94609
        www.newharbinger.com

The illustration at the start of chapter 11 borrows from a photograph by Sharon McCutcheon, available on Unsplash (unsplash.com).

Cover design by Catherine Adam and Katharine Hall

Illustrated by Katharine Hall/Kat Hall Creative

Interior layout and design by Catherine Bird/Wonderbird Photography and Design Studio

Acquired by Tesilya Hanauer

Edited by Karen Levy

Library of Congress Cataloging-in-Publication Data

Names: Ciarrochi, Joseph, author. | Hayes, Louise L., author. | Hall, Katharine (Illustrator), illustrator.
Title: Your life, your way : skills to help teens gain perspective, manage emotions, and build resilience using
    acceptance and commitment therapy / Joseph V. Ciarrochi & Louise L. Hayes ; illustrated by Katharine Hall.
Description: Oakland, CA : Instant Help, an imprint of New Harbinger Publications, Inc., [2020]
Identifiers: LCCN 2020009890 (print) | LCCN 2020009891 (ebook) | ISBN 9781684034659 (trade paperback) |
    ISBN 9781684034666 (pdf) | ISBN 9781684034673 (epub)
Subjects: LCSH: Youth--Life skills guides. | Youth--Mental health. | Emotions in adolescence.
Classification: LCC HQ796 .C473 2020 (print) | LCC HQ796 (ebook) | DDC 305.235--dc23
LC record available at https://lccn.loc.gov/2020009890
LC ebook record available at https://lccn.loc.gov/2020009891

Printed in the United States of America

22   21   20

10   9   8   7   6   5   4   3   2   1   First Printing

DEDICATION

To my daughter Grace, the teenager who teaches me about flexible strength and courage. To my son Vincent, the ten-year-old who reminds me to play and imagine. And, to my best friend Ann, whose strength, support, and love make me want to be strong, supportive, and loving.

—J.C.

To Mingma, for taking our long journey of steps, *bistārī*, *bistārī* (slowly, slowly). I am deeply honored to bask in your kindness and to watch you share this kindness every day, with everyone. Thank you for so many "cry-happy" moments of awe and wonder. To my sons Jackson and Darcy, you have made my life richer than I ever dreamed was possible. I am fortunate that as you've grown into men, you've become my friends.

—L.H.

CONTENTS

Acknowledgments vii

INTRODUCTION / HOW TO USE THIS BOOK 1

» **PART 1** / BUILDING YOUR SKILLS 5

Chapter 1   Let Your Heart Guide Your Journey 7

Chapter 2   Take Control of Your Life 15

                 Noticer: Hear the Messages in Your Body 22

                 Advisor: Use Your Inner Voice 27

                 Discoverer: Do, Test, and Build Experience 33

Chapter 3   Transform Your Viewpoint, Transform Your World 41

» **PART 2** / FOCUSING YOUR SKILLS 49

Chapter 4   When You Can't Stop Thinking or Worrying 51

Chapter 5   When You Are Anxious or Nervous 61

Chapter 6   Build Strong, Supportive Relationships 73

Chapter 7   Manage Bullies 87

Chapter 8   When You Feel Low or Sad 99

Chapter 9   When You Have Been Hurt, Been Afraid, or Feel Unsafe ... 111

Chapter 10 When Your Online Life Is a Hassle 117

Chapter 11 Develop Authentic Self-Confidence 129

Chapter 12 Become Excellent at Anything 141

Afterword 153

Dial into Your DNA-V Strengths 154

Resources & References 155

ACKNOWLEDGMENTS

We extend our gratitude to:

Catherine Adam, from Wonderbird Photography & Design Studio. Your inspirational design work and sharing of ideas is a gift that you offer so willingly. Thank you for sharing this with us.

Katharine Hall, from Kat Hall Creative. Kat, your illustrations brought our words to life and have made the message alive for the young people we serve. Thank you for being so willing to hear our crazy ideas and turn them into images with apparent ease.

We would also like to thank the young people who inspire and share their struggles with us. You teach us so much.

Thank you to our colleagues and friends across the world. You are too numerous to mention, but for this book we need to give special thanks to: Ben Sedley for his openness in sharing. The staff at New Harbinger, especially Tesilya Hanauer for her guidance, Vicraj Gill for helping the manuscript take good shape, and copy editor Karen Levy for her careful editing with teenagers in mind. Thank you to our families and friends for their encouragement, support, and, most of all, patience. And finally, this work would not exist without the original 1999 ACT book written by Steven Hayes, Kirk Strosahl, and Kelly Wilson, and the ongoing support and sharing from the community at the Association for Contextual Behavioral Science.

HOW TO READ THIS BOOK

*We have come here to let you know that change
is coming whether you like it or not.* / Greta Thunberg, teenage climate activist

Change can be hard for us humans; we like things to stay the same. You, however, have some say over how you change. Imagine you have been friends with someone for five years and then they betray you. You don't *want* this change; you could resist it, and pretend that nothing happened. But then you're just opening yourself up to more betrayal. You could also *choose* to change; you could escape your friend, get help, or confront your friend.

During change, some people grow strong, connected, and successful; others fall apart. This book will help you learn how to grow strong. It will show you how to turn change into your greatest source of strength. Not only will you learn to not fear change but you'll also learn how to embrace it and scream, **"Bring it on!"**

Greta Thunberg, teenage climate activist, is one example of how to use change to improve. When she was young, she found out about climate change and fell into a deep depression. *What can one girl do?* she thought. Then, Greta faced the change. She began to fight to protect the climate by sitting outside parliament with a handwritten sign that said, "School strike for climate." She wasn't an expert at change when she started. But

she kept showing up, persisting, and learning. She became stronger, wiser, and more effective. Eventually, because of her efforts, she sparked youth from all over the globe to demonstrate and demand governments prevent global warming. She was then nominated for a Nobel Peace Prize and featured on the cover of Time magazine. All by age sixteen. Greta never knew what would happen. She just started the change process with one small action—holding up a sign.

Some people never learn how to face change, and over time they become miserable adults. For example, some adults burn out in a job they hate; others become addicted to alcohol or gambling. Some give up their dreams and drop out; others sit at home, watching endless TV to distract themselves from their loneliness. You'll what they weren't able to; you'll learn to choose your path to an awesome life.

This book is about <u>your journey of change</u>, a journey to develop into the person you hope to be. You'll learn to create *your life, your way* by following these key steps:

» LET YOUR HEART GUIDE YOUR JOURNEY

To manage change and hardship, first get to know yourself: what you care about, what you value. You must know what kind of person you want to become. Then you'll discover a strength you didn't know you had. **You will find your passion, energy, and drive to overcome anything.**

You might find it hard to trust your heart, because other people tell you what you "should" do and feel. Don't worry, this book will help you find your answers. <u>You'll decide who you'll become with all of your heart.</u>

YOUR LIFE YOUR WAY
=
» **Let your heart guide your journey**

» **Embrace change**

» **Develop your flexible strength**

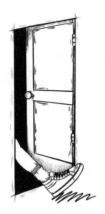

» EMBRACE CHANGE

Your life journey will involve constant change. Your world will change. And you'll change. Even now, you're changing. Your body is surging with electricity, with signals passing between your brain, heart, lungs, and muscles. This is happening right now, in your body. Neurons fire thoughts across your brain as you read these words: *Imagine a purple octopus wearing a cowboy hat.* Maybe now you're smiling; and when you smile, electricity jumps from one cell in your body to the next.

Let's do a quick exercise to see how easy it is to transform yourself. Imagine yourself:

Being strong
Being weak
Moving fast
Resting
Being helpful
Laughing

You are always transforming. The process of weight lifting illustrates this point. When you lift weights, you get stronger. The moment you stop, you get weaker. And if you avoid lifting any weight, your muscles will get too weak to lift anything. So too with living your life. As you study a subject, you get cleverer at it. Your brain changes and forms new connections between neurons. But if you were to stop studying altogether, and say, binge on TV for an entire year, you would lose your cleverness. Use it or lose it. Embrace change and you'll grow stronger.

» DEVELOP YOUR FLEXIBLE STRENGTH

Being able to embrace change requires *flexible strength*. This is the ability to persist in your journey when it's bringing you value and vitality, and change your direction when what you're doing is not bringing value.

For example, let's say you're in a romantic relationship and you're always fighting with your partner. You want to save the relationship, so you and your partner try to work through things. This involves having difficult conversations and sharing your deepest hopes and fears. But what if nothing stops the fighting? Do you persist in the difficult conversations? Or do you change direction, and walk away?

Flexible strength involves the ability to persist in the relationship when it builds value and walk away when it doesn't. **Flexible strength will help you live *your life, your way*.**

We base the flexible strength skills taught in this book on evidence from mindfulness-based interventions, acceptance and commitment therapy (ACT) interventions, and positive psychology interventions. We call the method DNA-V (this acronym stands for discoverer, noticer, advisor, values). This approach is about helping you optimize the skills you were born with—your ability to think, feel, and act in ways that help you focus on what matters and get more of what you want in life.

We have designed this book with your busy life in mind.

PART ONE of the book—**Building Your Skills**—will provide you with the foundation lessons that will help you turn your life in the direction you choose.

PART TWO of the book—**Focusing Your Skills**—will help you focus on particular issues you're likely face in life. These include things like what to do when you feel anxious, when you experience depressed mood, when you're trying to achieve, or when you have trouble with friends or bullies.

You can read the whole book, but you don't need to read from start to finish to benefit from it. Just read part 1, "Building Your Skills." Once you have finished that, you can jump to a chapter that interests you and start reading from there. Each chapter—once you've read the skills-building chapters—is self-contained.

You are ready to begin.

The daring adventure of life!

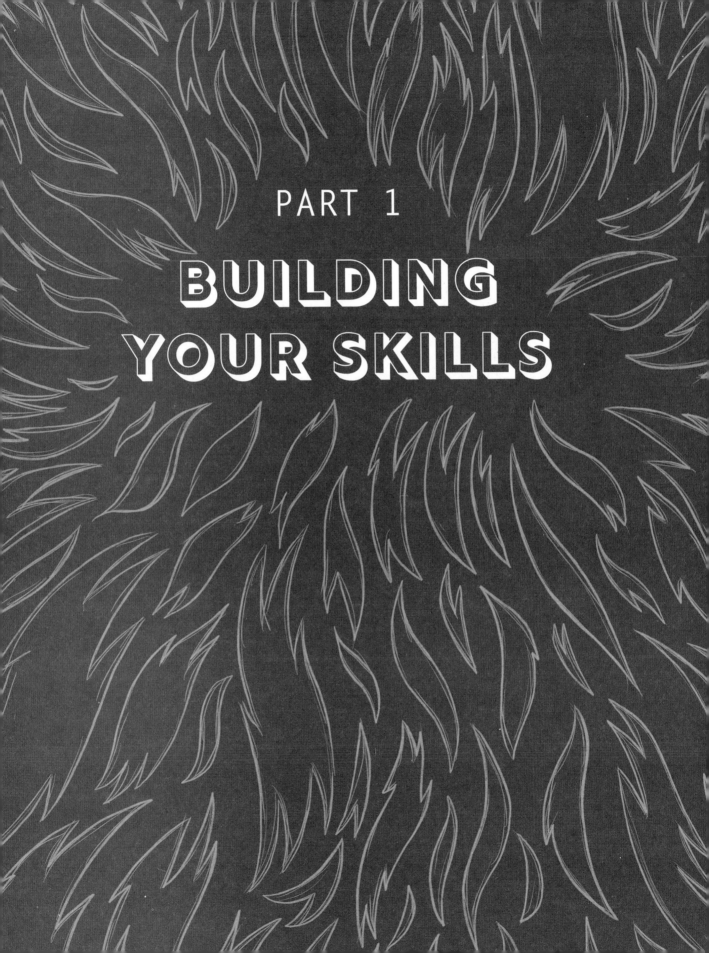

PART 1

BUILDING YOUR SKILLS

CHAPTER 1

LET YOUR HEART GUIDE YOUR JOURNEY

It is our choices, Harry, that show what we truly are,
far more than our abilities. / J.K. Rowling, *Harry Potter and the Chamber of Secrets*

So you're ready to start this great journey called life. What do you want? What direction do you want your life to go in? This first chapter will help you answer that question.

Remember as a kid when you daydreamed? Maybe you imagined yourself as an astronaut, flying high above the Earth and seeing our little blue dot in space. Maybe you became a famous celebrity and hung out in a two-hundred-room mansion, rolling around on the grass with your English sheepdog named Zappa. Perhaps you dreamed of becoming a great leader, an inventor, an explorer, or something else awesome.

Dreams aren't just kid stuff. Those big daydreams of yours, in some form, are the foundation for your life, your way. But they can also just fade away if you don't keep them alive.

Let's talk about adults who don't keep their dreams alive. They end up in a place we call **"Zombieland."** The colors are dull, nothing new happens, and people walk the streets mindlessly from one duty to the next. Occasionally, you see people with something other than tiredness in their eyes, maybe hope or excitement, as they think about escaping Zombieland during their two-week vacation. Maybe you've seen them become sad as they listen to the music of their adolescence, a time of intensity and passion. Here's the deal. Many in Zombieland never imagined they'd become so trapped, and yet they don't escape (they could!). They're afraid, so they stay there.

There's another place you can live; Zombieland isn't the only future.

ZOMBIELAND

You can also go to **Vitalityland**. Sure, it's a stupid name, but at least you know it's better than Zombieland. Adults in Vitalityland are dreamers and they are around us everywhere. Living in Vitalityland doesn't mean you need to be rich or famous; in fact, often the rich end up in Zombieland. People in Vitalityland follow what they love. Some write books or a secret journal. Others climb mountains or walk in their local park. Maybe they invent new things or tinker in their shed. Some protest by knitting yarn bombs to dazzle their city; others become excellent at sports or learning. Whatever they do, these crazy ones have the secret—they live life *their way*. They've learned to build their flexible strength, to act on their dreams, and to stop doing actions that don't build value. They know the power of dreaming.

Vitalityland

You stand between the dreams of Vitalityland and nightmares of Zombieland. You will come to know the path to Zombieland, as all humans do. We all become a "sleep walker" sometimes, losing sight of what is most important. This chapter will teach you how to recognize when you are drifting into Zombieland and how to stay on the path to Vitalityland.

Make no mistake, you can become one of the passionate, crazy ones in Vitalityland; someone fired up and driven. You can save the planet, change politics, create something beautiful, achieve excellence in sports or music, make other people smile, or become the best maker of surfboards on the earth. **Your life your way**.

» CHOOSING TO CARE

What is "your way"? Answer that question and you take the first step on the path to Vitalityland. Your path is unique.

The path to Zombieland is not unique. It's the same for everyone. The path to Zombieland involves being too afraid to dream. It involves getting yourself into "nots." That is, doing things to not displease others, not feel guilty and afraid, and *not* risk embarrassment and disappointment. You can't build a vital life with "nots."

To get yourself out of "nots," learn to say yes. You leave the zombie path the moment you say, Yes, I choose to care about something. **Yes, I will put my heart and soul into it**.

» OPENING THE DOOR

Let yourself think about the following questions (you might also discuss these questions with someone you trust).

1.   What would you do if you could live with no fear or doubt?

2.   If we gave you a secret key that opened the door to an amazing life, what would you be doing...

     » with your work or study?
     » with your relationships?
     » with new opportunities?

3.   What about right now? If you could finish tomorrow thinking it had been a good day, what things would you have done?

If you thought about these questions, you have taken the first step. Well done. If not, guess what? Keep reading and you're still opening that door to your path. Small steps matter.

» CHANGING YOUR LIFE USING THE SIX STEPS TO WELL-BEING

Generally, there are six types of activities that give you energy and wellbeing. They help you build vitality and create value—what we, throughout this book, will call your V. Flip this page to check them out and see if you identify activities you would like to try out in the coming weeks. Throughout this book you can come back to these six ways whenever you want to expand on your V.

1. Giving to others and having a positive influence.

You may find it hard to believe that giving to others promotes your own well-being, but it does. Think of times when you did something for someone, such as thanking someone, paying someone a compliment, or helping someone work through a problem. Or maybe you gave someone a gift by just listening to or accepting that person. Other ways of giving include taking care of animals or the environment.

Write some new ways you might give.

_____

_____

_____

_____

_____

2. Being active.

This includes exercise and sports, such as running, bicycling, weight lifting, playing tennis, or dancing. It also involves more moderate forms of activity and movement, such as walking or stretching. Think about some times when you've enjoyed physical activity or found it meaningful.

Write some new ways you might be active.

_____

_____

_____

_____

_____

3. Embracing the moment.

Think of times when you've paid attention with your five senses: touch, taste, sight, sound, and smell. Maybe you were noticing something in nature, experiencing the flavor of something, or listening to music. Or maybe you were fully mindful of a friend. Think of times when you've paid attention to something or someone with openness and curiosity.

Write some new ways you might you embrace the moment.

_____

_____

_____

_____

_____

4. Challenging yourself and learning.

Think of how you might challenge yourself or perhaps learn something new. What are some challenging activities that you find enjoyable, meaningful, or important?

Write some new ways you might challenge yourself and learn.

_____

_____

_____

_____

_____

5. Caring for yourself.

Self-care includes anything you do to make sure your mind and body are working well. Examples include treating yourself to a fun activity after a hard day at school, being kind to yourself during tough times, eating well, and getting enough sleep. People often put self-care last on their list—something they'll get to when they finish the other "important" tasks. However, self-care supports everything else we do, so it's worth devoting time to it.

Write some new ways you might care for yourself.

_____

_____

_____

_____

_____

6. Connecting with others.

This might involve family, friends, neighbors, and so on. Think about valued times you've had with other people.

Write some new ways you might connect with others.

_____

_____

_____

_____

_____

YOUR LIFE YOUR WAY

» LET YOUR HEART GUIDE YOUR JOURNEY

Your next steps are to not put this book in the bottom drawer. That's it.

People travel to Zombieland when life scares them. It sounds like a terrible place, doesn't it? We all end up in Zombieland sometimes. We all lose our way and forget who we are and what we love.

But Zombieland has no walls. If you end up there, by accident, then you can leave. Just start caring and act. Say, "Right now, I choose to care."

Do you want to care in this moment?

» EMBRACE CHANGE

Remember, the way to Zombieland involves being too afraid to dream. Dreams are scary, risky things. Will you succeed or fail? Will you find love when you ask someone out, or will someone reject you? **Every dream has its risks**. But if you're unwilling to risk, then you end up on *that* path, the one that leads to a dead end: a small, unfulfilled life.

Read on to learn about developing the mental skills you need to embrace change and grow stronger.

Continued on the next page

» DEVELOP YOUR FLEXIBLE STRENGTH

For the next week, practice noticing when you are feeling discouraged, bored, or unmotivated. Then flip the "caring" switch. Choose to care about something in that exact moment. You might choose to care about one of the six ways to well-being: connecting, giving, being active, embracing the moment, challenging yourself, and caring for yourself. Each moment is a new opportunity to create your life, your way.

CHAPTER 2

TAKE CONTROL OF YOUR LIFE

You're both the fire and the water that extinguishes it. You're the narrator, the protagonist, and the sidekick. You're the storyteller and the story told. You are somebody's something, but you are also your you.

/ John Green, *Turtles All the Way Down*

Y ou can be many different characters in the story you call your life. You can act like a person who is strong, weak, courageous, silly, serious, outgoing, shy, kind, or mean. It's up to you. The point is, you can change how you act and view the world. This is your superpower and your key to developing flexible strength, the ability to persist in your journey even when you encounter problems and unhelpful people. If you develop flexible strength, you will be ready to handle any difficulties life throws at you.

You can see the world through many different viewpoints. Here is a quick exercise to illustrate how you can switch from one viewpoint to another. Imagine you have volunteered to be in a play. You get assigned to play a shy character. Imagine you're that character. How might you see other people? Does the shy character see other people as threatening?

Write some ideas below.

_____

_____

_____

_____

_____

_____

_____

Now imagine you get assigned to be a powerful and nasty character. How might this character see people? Does the nasty character hurt other people? How?

Write some ideas below.

_____

_____

_____

_____

_____

_____

_____

_____

» WHY WE GET STUCK

You know you're stuck if you keep doing the same thing and keep getting the same bad results. For example, imagine someone named Sebastian wants to make friends, but he fears being judged by others. He thinks, *What if they don't like me? What if they think I'm stupid?* To cope with his anxiety, he goes to the library and works by himself in a cubicle hidden behind the stacks of books. He feels safe. But the next day he feels even more worried about what others think, so he goes to the library again. He doesn't try something different. Sebastian is doing the same thing repeatedly and making his life worse. Sebastian is stuck.

Here is another example. Hanna wants to do well in math, but math makes her anxious. So she procrastinates and avoids studying. This helps her not feel anxious today. But what happens tomorrow? She feels even more anxious because she hasn't studied and she fails the test. If she keeps procrastinating, her life will just get worse.

Sebastian and Hanna aren't broken. Getting stuck is normal for humans. You'll see that chapters 4 to 12 of this book are all about getting unstuck from problems and hassles that happen in life and becoming the best version of you that you can be.

WHAT GETTING STUCK LOOKS LIKE

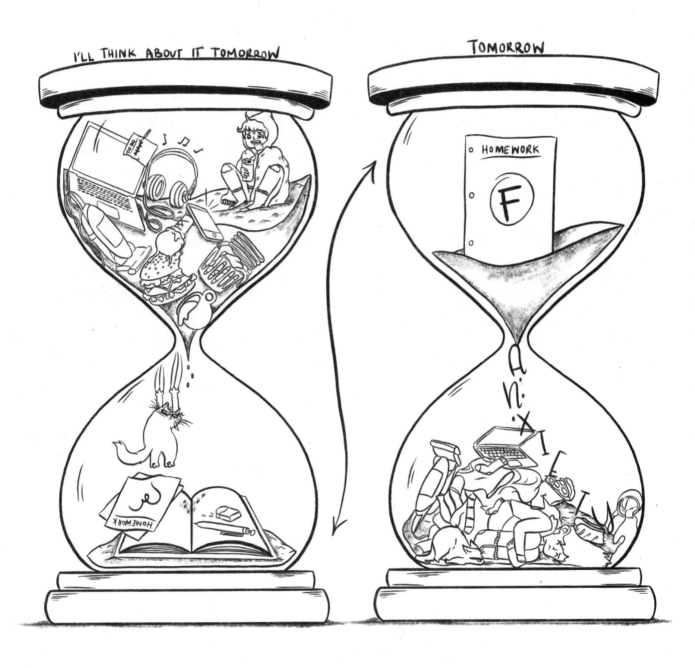

Getting stuck means that we have a problem and the way we try to fix it doesn't work. There are lots of ways we get stuck. It's also hard for most of us to see that this is happening. Here are a few examples. **Which ones are most familiar to you?**

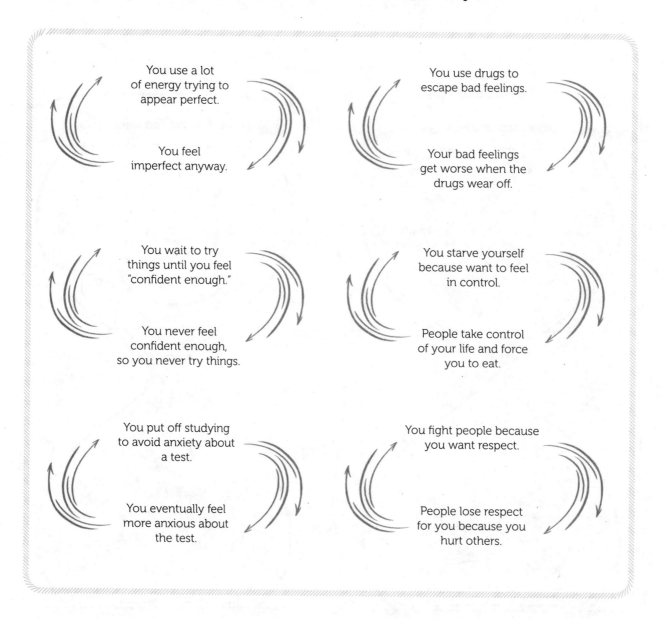

You use a lot of energy trying to appear perfect.

You feel imperfect anyway.

You use drugs to escape bad feelings.

Your bad feelings get worse when the drugs wear off.

You wait to try things until you feel "confident enough."

You never feel confident enough, so you never try things.

You starve yourself because want to feel in control.

People take control of your life and force you to eat.

You put off studying to avoid anxiety about a test.

You eventually feel more anxious about the test.

You fight people because you want respect.

People lose respect for you because you hurt others.

You'll get stuck sometimes. We all do. It's just human. The key question is, How do we get unstuck? How do we restart the positive process of growth and change?

Getting Unstuck by Switching Viewpoints

Now, we're ready to learn the DNA switching skills that are essential for flexible strength. We are going to learn to switch between being a discoverer (or doer), a noticer, and an advisor (or thinker). To apply these viewpoint shifts, we will focus on a specific challenge in your life, one for which you might be stuck. Then we will show you how to switch up your DNA viewpoints to get unstuck in that situation.

Ready to live your life, your way?

Here is a list of common challenges that many young people experience at some point. Pick one of these challenges you want to work on.

- » **Inner concerns:** Feeling conflicted about what to do, regret over past decisions
- » **Physical appearance:** Concerns that your body is not good enough
- » **Time pressure:** Having too many things to do, too much responsibility, or not enough time for fun
- » **School/college/work challenges:** Being dissatisfied with school or college, unhappy at your work, or hassled by teachers or bosses
- » **Family challenges:** Conflict or struggles with family members
- » **Worry about the future:** Thinking a lot about what will happen and fearing bad things
- » **Relationship challenges:** Difficulties with friends or romantic relationships

Let's do some writing. It might not seem like fun to write about a challenge, but research shows that expressive writing helps us take new perspectives and grow. You'll work through your selected challenge in this chapter.

Take some time and write about the challenge you're facing. Think about specific times that the challenge occurred and your deepest emotions and thoughts related to it. Aim for 10 minutes of expressive writing, completing these sentences as you go:

The challenge I'm facing is...

_____

_____

_____

_____

My feelings about this are...

_____

_____

_____

_____

My thoughts about this are...

_____

_____

_____

_____

Now write how you would like this challenging situation to be resolved. What outcome would you most want? (Dream big!)

My ideal outcome is...

_____

_____

_____

Outcomes are important in life, but you cannot always guarantee getting the exact outcome you want. For example, if you want someone to treat you kindly, you might act kindly toward them, but you cannot guarantee they will return this kindness. The one thing you have control over is your own behavior. You can decide to act consistently with what *you* value, no matter what the rest of the world does. The good news is this: when you act consistently with your values, you're giving yourself the best chance to get the outcome you want.

So, let's find the value behind your challenge. Here are some example words that suggest what you might value: *being strong, assertive, kind, honorable, caring, fun, supportive, friendly, agreeable, bold, persistent, trying again, giving, being active, enjoying the moment.* Now write about what values you want your actions to demonstrate.

In this challenging situation, I want to be a person who...

_____

_____

_____

_____

My value is...

_____

_____

_____

Now that you have a sense of how you want to be in this situation, you're ready to explore your challenging situation through three different viewpoints: **the discoverer**, **the noticer**, and **the advisor** (DNA). Each of the three sections that follow will develop your DNA skills. Then we'll ask you to apply each skill to the challenging situation you identified above. **Let's make your first viewpoint switch.**

» NOTICER: HEAR THE MESSAGES IN YOUR BODY

When you switch viewpoints, you can switch anywhere, into noticer, discoverer, or advisor. Here, we will start with the noticer switch.

The noticer skill is the ability to observe what's going on around you and inside you. You experience the world through your body—that is, through your feelings and through touch, taste, sound, hearing, and smell. When you're using your noticer, it's like you're experiencing a scene but not always reacting to it. For example, you might experience your own feelings coming and going, and not react to them unless you *choose* to. Or you might witness how a friend's facial expression changes as you reveal a secret.

Noticer is the skill you have from the moment you're born. It's the skill you'll return to until your last breath. As a baby, you noticed what went on around you and inside you. You noticed the sensations of your body and screamed when you felt hungry or cold. You noticed safety and danger too. It didn't take you long to fall in love when you looked into the eyes of someone you loved, or to feel fear when you looked into a stranger's eyes. As you grew, you came to notice the feeling of grass between your toes, the sound of leaves blowing in the wind, and your delight at the cat appearing on the fence. All these experiences were building your noticer skill.

Now you're much older and you notice so many things every day. Wouldn't you want to sharpen this skill so you can harness it? Your noticer is always present, but sometimes we forget that. Let's do a little exercise to connect with your noticer skill now.

THE NOTICER

Meet Your Noticer

1. Notice your feet in your shoes. Wriggle your toes just to be sure they're there.

2. Notice five fast breaths. Notice five slow breaths.

3. Notice three white things around you.

Each one of these is using your noticer viewpoint. If you can do these—and you can—you already have what you need. Now it's time to become even more skilled at being a noticer. First, consider how you use this skill right now.

Are Your Noticer Skills Letting You Down?

Noticer is such a simple skill. It's so simple we often forget about it. Let's look at how you're using your noticer skills now. Use the chart to see how skilled you are with your noticer. **Check the items that describe you.**

Your Noticer Skills

Helpful Noticer Activity	Unhelpful Noticer Activity
☐ I'm aware of sensations in my body.	☐ I don't know what is going on inside my body.
☐ I can pause and slow myself down.	☐ I overreact to things.
☐ I can describe my feelings.	☐ I struggle to describe my feelings.
☐ I allow all my feelings, even the negative ones.	☐ I hate my negative feelings and want them to go away.
☐ I notice how other people feel.	☐ I have no idea what others are feeling.
☐ I am good at noticing what is going on in the current moment.	☐ I get lost inside my head and don't notice what's going on around me.
☐ I can ground myself when I have strong feelings.	☐ I hurt myself or do something unhelpful when I have strong feelings.

How did you do? If you checked mostly helpful strategies, then you're good at using your noticer already. You can still sharpen this skill, though. This is a lifelong task.

Noticing skills are crucial to your everyday life. Think of yourself as a car driver and your emotions as traffic signals. If you don't see the signals, you end up having a serious accident. Have you ever reacted badly to your emotions? Maybe you were angry one time, but you didn't realize you were angry until you'd lashed out. Too late. You've crashed through the emotion and now have a wreckage to clean up.

When you learn to use your noticer well, you become aware of anger, and then you have choices. (Not always, but often.) You might still retaliate, but you might also confront the person who made you angry, or perhaps just ignore the incident.

Consider test anxiety, which is like a sneaky emotion signal. Maybe you don't see it, and you just tell yourself that you don't *want* to study for that test. When you practice noticing your anxiety, you realize that you *do care* about doing well on the test. Ignoring your anxiety has worked against your goal of getting good grades. Too late, again. If you sharpen your noticer, you can choose to study, or you can choose to procrastinate. <u>The important thing is this: you choose.</u>

How to Improve Your Noticer

Skilled noticing involves learning how to notice and understand what we experience and feel, knowing that feelings can't overwhelm us when we notice them. Noticing should be easy. Babies can do it. But skilled noticing becomes difficult for us overthinking and threat-sensitive humans.

Emotions are like text messages or social media messages you receive on your phone. What do you do when you get a message you don't like—do you smash the phone against the wall? What about if you get a confusing or disappointing message— does that mean there's something wrong with your phone? Do you demand a new phone No.? You do none of these things. You don't blame your phone for the mixed or unpleasant messages. Why, then, would you blame yourself for having unpleasant emotional signals? You might even think, "What is wrong with me. Why do I feel so... [insert the emotion you least like]?"

To strengthen your noticer skill, you need to remember two things:

1. **Accept:** Accept that all feelings are normal. A lot of times, what you care about (such as success) naturally brings up difficult feelings (such as fear of failure). So, the more you care about stuff, the more you'll need to accept and make space for difficult feelings. These feelings are like messages on your phone. Messages won't break your phone, and feelings won't break you.

2. **Act:** Act by using a three-step noticer practice:
    » Awareness of your breath. Take a few slow, deep breaths and ground yourself.
    » Center your awareness on what is inside your body. Scan your body for sensations (such as tension in your shoulders, butterflies in your stomach, lightheadedness, feeling hot).
    » Tell yourself how you feel. Can you label the sensations with a feeling label (such as sad, angry, anxious, nervous, tense, joyful, peaceful, guilty, ashamed)?

Everyday Practices for Sharpening Your Noticer

Noticer skills may sound new to you, but they aren't. You have been using your noticer for most of your life; you just didn't label it that way. The quiz below will help you think about fun ways to sharpen this skill.

The DNA Quick Quiz

How do you sharpen your noticer?

☐ I like to take photographs.

☐ I enjoy watching what other people do and how they interact.

☐ I like to experience things through dance, sport, or other kinds of movement.

☐ I like to be in nature.

☐ I enjoy tasting different foods.

☐ I'd like to be a chef someday.

☐ I'd like to direct films someday.

☐ I'd like to be a tour guide someday.

☐ I like to just hang out and appreciate what is around me.

Below, write your favorite three activities from the list. Then add other noticer activities that you do that aren't on this list.

_____

_____

_____

_____

_____

Apply the Noticer to Your Challenging Situation

Take a moment to think about the challenge you chose to focus on earlier in the chapter. Imagine it's happening now, that you're engaging in it.

Now choose your *accept* and *act* steps.

To strengthen your noticer skill, you need to remember two things:

1. **Accept:**
   Can you accept and make space for the difficult feelings? (Yes/No)

   If you answered no, don't worry. We will work on acceptance skills throughout the book.

   If you answered yes, great! You're strengthening your noticer skill each time you do this.

2. **Act:**
   We call this the "ACT Centering Exercise." It is something you can do anytime you feel like you are stuck, overwhelmed, or like you might do something you will regret.

ACT Centering Exercise

Awareness of your breath. Just notice. Maybe take a few slow breaths. No need to rush.

Center your awareness in your body. When you think about your challenge, what sensations do you notice?

Tell yourself how you feel.

Take notice of what is happening around you right now. For example, you may deliberately notice and name five things around you. Notice five things you hear.

When you switch to your noticer, you sense what is going on in your body and watch your emotions rising and falling. And if you sharpen your noticer skills, you can learn that your emotions—or other people's emotions—need not push you around. You can watch your feelings with curiosity, and learn to respond with awareness.

Noticer is an awesome space, but we wouldn't want to stay there forever. There are many ways to view life. Let's get into a new viewpoint now.

THE ADVISOR

» ADVISOR: USE YOUR INNER VOICE

Advisor is the skill of telling yourself what is good and bad, what to do, and how to fix problems.

The advisor is the name we give to our inner voice. You might think of your advisor as a character, sitting on your shoulder, whispering in your ear. This character would look a bit like you (because it's a part of you).

Some things your advisor might tell you include:
"It will work out if you keep trying."
"You're too tired to do any more studying."
"Hide your feelings."
"Come on, you can do it."
"Don't trust that person."

There are many other sources of advice, such as parents, teachers, and friends. Even the artificial intelligence on your phone gives you advice. But inside you, there's just one advisor—it's your own unique voice. As you grew and learned, your advisor took in all of the information that surrounded you and turned that into self-advice. So now, here you are, living your life with your own voice telling you what you should do. Sounds wild, doesn't it?

The advisor is one of the most amazing human skills. The more your advisor learns, the more you can use it to help you in any situation.

Meet Your Advisor

Imagine you step into the room next door from where you're reading this, and you see a koala, a nice furry ball, sitting in your desk chair. You've never experienced that before, right?

Name the first two thoughts you might have when you see this koala. This is your advisor speaking. We expect your advisor will immediately help you out by asking questions like:

1. What is that furry thing?
2. Why is it here?
3. How did it get in?
4. What should I do about it?
5. Should I poke it or call wildlife rescue?
6. Are koalas dangerous?
7. Is this a joke?
8. Is someone playing a trick on me?

All of this will happen in seconds. And then your advisor is likely to figure out escape routes, reasoning about what koalas can and can't do.

Your advisor can be useful for helping you figure out what to do in any situation, whether it's an evil koala, a math problem, a fight with a friend, or a million other things in everyday life. For example, you can say to yourself:

"Get out of bed and get to work."

OR

"Don't get out of bed; work is not important."

Your advisor can also give you advice about how you should act, such as:

"Don't talk too much; people won't like you."

OR

"Don't say that to your friend, she'll get mad at you."

As you can tell, your advisor's advice isn't always helpful. Thus, your job isn't to always obey your advisor or to get mad at it. Your task is to learn when to listen to it.

Are Your Advisor Skills Letting You Down?

Can you think of times when you were stuck inside your head, criticizing yourself and worrying excessively about something? How about a time when you couldn't sleep because you kept remembering something bad that happened during the day? That's your advisor out of control. Let's do a quick self-awareness exercise to recognize helpful and unhelpful advisor behavior.

Look at the advisor activities in the table below. **Which ones did you do recently?**

Your Advisor Skills

Helpful Advisor Activity	Unhelpful Advisor Activity
☐ I used problem solving to improve my life.	☐ I worried too much.
☐ I thought about the past so I could learn from my mistakes.	☐ I couldn't stop thinking about the past.
☐ I thought about how I could improve at something.	☐ I criticized myself a lot.
☐ I could notice when my thinking was not helping me (too much worry or self-criticism, or dwelling on the past).	☐ I wasted a lot of time thinking about stuff that was unimportant.
☐ I told myself helpful things like, "There are reasons for people to like me" or "keep trying."	☐ I told myself unhelpful things like, "I'm worthless" or "I have no hope."

Because you spend so much time using your advisor skill (we all do), you might even use it too much. You can tell you're stuck with your advisor if you can't stop worrying or thinking about something bad in the past. Sometimes, just noticing you're overusing your advisor can be the first step to getting unstuck.

YOUR INNER ADVISOR IS ALWAYS WHISPERING TO YOU.

How to Improve Your Advisor

Here are some simple things you can do to strengthen your advisor skill. Once again, you can remember them with the words *accept* and *act*.

1. **Accept:**
   » **Accept that the negative thoughts it gives you are just your advisor doing its job.** The advisor is like a threat-detection machine; its job is to work out what is wrong and fix it. Your advisor won't be able to fix things if it's always thinking about rainbows and unicorns. Its job is to keep you safe, not make you think happy thoughts constantly.

   » **Accept that your advisor has to work all the time.** Wouldn't it be great if you could turn off your advisor when it's negative? The problem is then you'd have no threat-detection system—you'd just have rainbows and unicorns in your head. What do you think would happen next? You would die as soon as you walked out on a busy road because you'd have no ability to say to yourself, *Hey watch out!* The reality is you can't turn off your advisor. Turn the page and see for yourself...

Take 20 seconds to focus on your breath and nothing else. Notice when your advisor appears (this is when you think about this task or something else) and then try to return to your breath. Ready, begin.

--------------- *Begin timing now* ---------------

» Now consider what happened. Did your thoughts wander? Did you hear your advisor coming through, making judgments and evaluations? Everybody's mind wanders because you, and everybody else, has an advisor that's always looking for problems. So, don't try to shut down your advisor. You can't win that battle.

» **Accept that you can't erase the past.** Is one challenge you're facing something that happened in the past? Did you make a mistake or have a bad experience with a friend? When we have a bad memory, it's tempting to want to erase it. It seems like that's the logical thing to do. But, if you could erase memories, here's what might happen:

You go to school and a bully kicks you in the head. The memory is so bad that you go home, get out your magic advisor eraser, and wipe out the memory. That night you sleep soundly—great! But then, the next day, you go to school and you don't avoid that bully. You get kicked in the head again. And this repeats every day.

If that seems like some crazy cartoon, you're right. Fortunately, or unfortunately, we don't forget things in the past. We can't erase them, because if we could we would be dead. This means if you're attempting to erase a bad memory, your brain and your biology are against you. You'll lose. (Don't panic, you can learn what to do for difficult memories in chapter 9.)

2. **Act:**

» **Act as if you're in charge, not your advisor (because you are!).** Use problem solving when it's useful. Stop using it when it's not useful (that is, when it is a lot of worry going nowhere). Don't believe everything your advisor tells you. You know that not everything people tell you is right or useful, don't you? The same is true for your advisor. It can offer a lot of unhelpful advice, such as, *You can't do it*, or *Just give up*, or *Don't trust anybody*. This self-talk isn't good or bad. It all depends on how you use it—what you do.

As you have gone through life, your advisor has made a rule book just for you. Maybe it includes negative rules like, *You suck at math*, or *You're not very popular*, or *You're not good enough*. Here's the thing: you can also create and test new rules anytime you want. You can use your advisor for good. For example, have you ever felt insecure about doing something but told yourself, *Come on, you can do it*? That's an example of you creating a new rule. You might have created a new rule like, *I might struggle with math* (or whatever), *but I'll try it anyway*. Here is one of the best advisor rules: <u>The advisor is not always right or useful.</u>

» **Act by switching up your DNA.** One of the simplest ways to practice becoming more skilled with your advisor is to "DNA switch" out of your advisor and into your noticer or discoverer skill. We don't have to stay stuck in our heads. We can notice what is around us (N) or we can do something enjoyable (D). It's easy to notice thoughts, but many of us forget that we're in charge, not our advisors. Go on, try it. Next time you're stuck, step into your noticer and connect yourself to whatever is around you, or step into your discoverer and try an action to help yourself.

Everyday Practices for Sharpening Your Advisor

Your advisor isn't a new, fancy thing; it's just a neat way of learning about how you can get flexible with your problem solving, self-limiting beliefs, and the things you tell yourself. The quiz below will help you think about sharpening this skill.

The DNA Quick Quiz

How do you sharpen your advisor?

☐ I like to organize my life.

☐ I like to argue my point.

☐ I like to figure things out.

☐ I like to follow instructions and build cool things.

☐ I like to solve problems.

☐ I like to be like a detective and investigate.

☐ I like to be like a lawyer and search for answers.

☐ I like discussing ideas with my friends.

☐ I like to anticipate problems and figure out ways to avoid them.

Write your favorite three activities from the list below. Then add other advisor activities that you do that aren't on the list..

_____

_____

_____

_____

_____

Apply the Advisor to Your Challenging Situation

Now you can sharpen your advisor skills. Return to the challenging situation you were working on before. Think about what difficult or negative thoughts show up for you when you're facing this issue. Write these thoughts below. Don't filter out thoughts you think are *bad* or *stupid*. Remember, all of us have advisors that tell us unhelpful things sometimes.

_____

_____

_____

_____

_____

_____

_____

_____

_____

_____

_____

Now, look at the *accept* and *act* steps in the "How to Improve Your Advisor" section a few pages back. Those steps show things you can do to get flexible with your advisor. Write one or two of your own *accept* and *act* ideas below. Consider these questions: What are you going to do if the difficult thoughts show up? Will you let them push you around? Can you let the thoughts come and go, without reacting to them? Can you do something you value, even when your advisor is discouraging you?

_____

_____

_____

_____

_____

_____

_____

When you are overthinking and your advisor is unhelpful, you can shift into noticer and just embrace the moment around you. Or you can shift into the discoverer. **Let's do that now.**

» DISCOVER: DO, TEST, AND BUILD EXPERIENCE

The discoverer is the part of you that does things in the world. It explores, tests things out, and uses trial and error to find the best path forward.

With a skilled discoverer, you learn to build independence. You learn you can *do things* that make your life better. You learn to make things happen in the world. Most of all, the discoverer helps you build relationships and expand your skills.

A good way to recall the discoverer is to consider how you learned to walk: you stood up, fell down, and stood up again. You kept trying until you could do it. That's how everyone learns to walk. There are many things you have learned using your discoverer, such as riding a bike, reading, solving math problems, even cutting your nails—the discoverer involves any action that requires making mistakes and trying again. It's the essence of how humans learn. There's a discoverer inside you just waiting to burst out.

However, being human, we don't always use our discoverer skillfully. Sometimes we just act out or do the same thing over and over even if the outcome is bad. We will help you learn how to harness your discoverer for good.

THE DISCOVERER

Meet Your Discoverer

Here are two ways you can meet your discoverer:

1. Do something, in this exact moment, that you have never done before. Maybe it's something silly, like standing on one foot while juggling two shirts. Maybe it's something as simple as doing a stretch or spinning in a circle. Don't worry about feeling stupid (that happens a lot in the discoverer space). Just do something new.

2. Pick something nice to do for another person, something you've never done. Do it. Watch how the person responds.

    What did you do? And how did the person respond?

    _____

    _____

    _____

Discoverer is a skill you use to build value in your life. Below is a list of six well-being activities. Pick one of them, or make up your own. Then do this activity in some new way in the next twenty-four hours.

Give

1. Donate time or money to charity.
2. Do something to improve the environment.
3. Cheer someone up.
4. Be kind to someone in need.
5. Help someone with work.
6. Take care of someone.

Embrace the Moment

1. Notice the world around you.
2. Enjoy a meal through all your senses (sight, sound, taste, smell, touch).
3. Pay full attention when talking to a friend or loved one.
4. Appreciate the small things that make your life better.
5. Observe a wild animal or pet for a short period.
6. Watch something occur in the physical world with curiosity (e.g., sunrise).

Be Active

1. Take a walk.
2. Play a sport.
3. Dance.
4. Exercise.
5. Swim.
6. Bicycle or skateboard.

Care for Yourself

1. Make sure you get enough sleep.
2. Eat vegetables and fruit.
3. Avoid eating too much junk.
4. Schedule time to relax.
5. Give yourself breaks between work.
6. Read, stretch, or do some other relaxing activity.

Challenge Yourself/ Learn

1. Learn to cook something.
2. Make something.
3. Learn a musical instrument.
4. Develop an athletic skill.
5. Take on a challenging but fun project.
6. Get better at your work.

Connect with Someone

7. Phone a friend.
8. Do something with family.
9. Visit someone.
10. Send a compliment via text.
11. Say something nice to someone you care about.
12. Enjoy a coffee or meal with someone.

What will you do?

_____

_____

_____

_____

_____

_____

_____

Are Your Discoverer Skills Letting You Down?

Toddlers are constantly trying different things: exploring, putting their nose in every new thing they see, dropping things off their high chair and watching a parent pick it up. Now, compare toddlers to older people. Have you noticed that some older people rarely try new things? You might hear them say things like, "That won't work. I know because I tried it in 1938." What do you think happened between the toddler years and their old age?

Well, for most people, we end up relying on our advisor and our past learning. We don't use our discoverer skills by trying things out—and risking failure. And when we stop discovering, we lose the ability to learn new behaviors and skills.

To get a sense of where you are at with your discoverer, consider the quiz below. Mark off all the ways you used your discoverer during the last few days.

Your Discoverer Skills

Helpful Discoverer Activity	Unhelpful Discoverer Activity
☐ I challenged myself to see if I could get better at something.	☐ I played it safe and didn't get better at something.
☐ I paid attention to whether or not my behavior created value and vitality in my life.	☐ I acted impulsively and made my life worse.
☐ I took a risk, and did something new, in order to improve my life.	☐ I did nothing new. I tried to avoid taking all risks and making any mistakes.
☐ I paid attention to the consequences of my actions.	☐ I didn't notice the consequences of my actions.

How did you do? If you didn't use your discoverer in a new way today, it's okay. This is normal. In the sections to come, we'll look at how you can.

How to Improve Your Discoverer

Being a skilled discoverer involves trying things and paying attention to whether it worked—that is, whether it improved your life. Here are some simple things you can do to strengthen your discoverer skill. Once again, you can remember them with the words *accept* and *act*.

1. **Accept:**

   » Accept that some things you do in your life don't make your life better. We all have bad habits.

   » Accept that trying new things can be distressing and difficult.

2. **Act:**

   » Act in new or different ways. Don't live in your comfort zone 100 percent of the time. Try new things: new ways of being active, interacting with others, challenging yourself, caring for yourself, giving and enjoying the moment.

   » Act according to what works. Pay attention. What happens after you do something new? Do you get the result you wanted? If not, try something else.

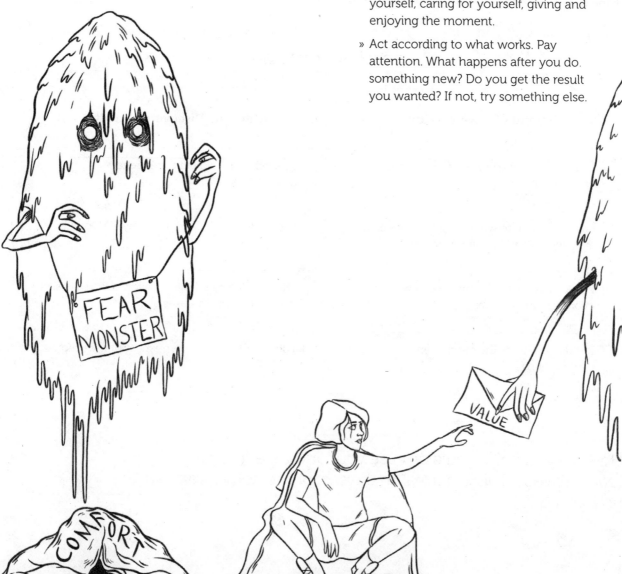

Everyday Practices for Sharpening Your Discoverer

You have been using your discoverer all your life; you just didn't label it that way. Take this quiz to show how you can strengthen it even more.

The DNA Quick Quiz

How do you sharpen your discoverer?

- ☐ I like to create things.
- ☐ I like to explore.
- ☐ I like to invent.
- ☐ I like to make art.
- ☐ I like to design things.
- ☐ I like to study new things.
- ☐ I like to travel and explore new places.
- ☐ I like to try new activities.
- ☐ I like to meet new people.
- ☐ I enjoy figuring things out by doing, rather than just thinking.

Write your favorite three activities from the list in the space below. Then add other discoverer activities you do that aren't on this list.

_____

_____

_____

_____

Apply the Discoverer to Your Challenging Situation

Now, return one last time to your challenging situation, and let's learn how to *accept* and *act* as a discoverer. Consider the following questions and write your answers in the space below.

1. **Accept:**

   » **Accept that some things you do are ineffective.** What do you typically do in your challenging situation?

   In my challenging situation, I typically do...

   _____

   _____

2. **Act:**

   » **Act in new ways.** Think about two things you don't usually do. These two new things don't have to sound logical, amazing, life changing, or anything like that, they just have to be things you don't usually do or haven't tried before. A big hint is to try things opposite to what you normally try. For example, if you usually argue a point, the opposite would be to try listening instead. Or, if you usually avoid a situation, the opposite would be to try putting yourself in the situation and trust that you can handle it.

   In my challenging situation, I'd like to try something new or different. I'd like to...

   _____

   _____

Now if you try something new, your advisor is likely to freak out and try to discourage you. Remember your advisor is often against new, unpredictable things, because its main job is to stop things from going wrong. You don't have to always listen to your advisor, though; you learn from your discoverer too.

   » **Act on what works.** A skilled discoverer tries different things and watches what happens next. In the space below, answer these questions: Did your new action work? Did it improve your situation, or make you better at something? If not, then don't do it again. If yes, then do more of it.

   _____

   _____

   _____

YOUR LIFE YOUR WAY

» LET YOUR HEART GUIDE YOUR JOURNEY

Why practice discoverer, noticer, and advisor skills? The answer is simple: these skills help you build a life that's filled with fun, adventure, and love.

» EMBRACE CHANGE

Don't run from change; face it and use it. You can transform yourself so that change does not break you. The image that follows summarizes how to do this. In the center of this disk is a "V dial." You can transform yourself by turning the dial toward discoverer, noticer, or advisor (DNA) to create more value (V) in your life.

» DEVELOP YOUR FLEXIBLE STRENGTH

Keep the image on the next page to remind yourself of how you can use DNA-V to face challenges and improve your life. Building strength involves practice, practice, practice. The more you practice transforming yourself, the more you develop flexible strength.

» <u>Discoverer:</u> Turn the dial to discoverer (**D**) to see if trying something new makes life better.

» <u>Noticer:</u> Turn the dial to noticer (**N**) to see if paying attention with curiosity and not reacting makes life better.

» <u>Advisor:</u> Turn the dial to advisor (**A**) to see if careful thinking and problem solving makes life better.

» This is what we mean by "DNA switching." If you feel stuck, DNA switch. Turn the dial toward the D, N, or A viewpoint that best helps you build value.

Using your DNA-V to create your life your way

Accept: Your typical behavior may not be working—that is, it isn't improving your skills or making your life the best it can be.

Accept: Your inner advisor is like a threat-detecting machine that can't be turned off.

Accept: Only by challenging yourself to do better will you get better. Be willing to fail in order to improve.

Accept: Your advisor can sometimes be negative. Your advisor is imperfect and doesn't know everything.

Act: Have faith. Act as if you can improve, even if your advisor says you can't.

Act: Don't fight the advisor. Don't believe everything your advisor says.

Remind yourself: What kind of person do you want to be? What do you care about? What do you love doing?

Act: Try something new or different. Notice if the new behavior works.

Act: Problem solve to create new advisor rules that help you.

Accept: Difficult feelings are normal and don't need to be eliminated. Valued activities often elicit positive and negative feelings.

Act: A: Awareness of breath (i.e., take a few slow breaths).

C: Center awareness on your body; notice sensations.

T: Tell yourself how you feel. Take notice of what is happening around you.

CHAPTER 3

TRANSFORM YOUR VIEWPOINT, TRANSFORM YOUR WORLD

Change will not come if we wait for some other person, or if we wait for some other time. We are the ones we've been waiting for. We are the change that we seek. / Barack Obama

Just as this quote implies, you are the one you are waiting for. In this chapter, you'll find yourself, find your self-worth, and discover your superpower to build friendships. You'll do this by strengthening your viewpoint skills.

Switching between Discoverer, Noticer and Advisor lets you experience the world in different ways. Step into advisor space, and you see the world as a problem to be solved. In the next image, a boy named Lee is seeing the long dive into the water as a potential problem. Step into discoverer space, and you take action, do things and find out what happens next. Lee becomes a discoverer when he dives off the board. Step into noticer space, and experience the world as images, sensations, sounds, smells, and feelings. Lee moves into noticer space when he lays on his back in the water and just experiences life.

EXPERIENCE THE WORLD...

Let's continue your DNA view a little further. You have the ability to see yourself being a discoverer, noticer, or advisor. Lee could do this by remembering his different experiences diving into the water. It's like he's scrolling through his phone through different pictures he took when he was being an advisor, a discoverer, and a noticer. **"Self-view"** lets you see that you are many possibilities.

"Self-view" also lets you "look at yourself" or imagine yourself in the past and the future. Can you remember when you did something amazing and new? Just see yourself doing that now. You're viewing yourself as a discoverer. Can you remember a time when you were trying to solve a problem? Imagine that now. You're viewing yourself as an advisor. You may think this is not important, but as you'll learn below, self-view is a big deal. Self-view holds the key to overcoming self-doubt and building your life, your way.

Finally, there's another viewpoint you can take. We call this **"social view."** Take this view, and you focus on other people, rather than yourself. You can try to see how they're thinking and feeling. You even guess what they intend to do. Social view is the key to making friends and managing bullies. In the below image, Lee is taking a social view when he imagines what his friend thinks of him diving.

Rather than talking more about self-view and social view, let's instead switch into them now.

» THE POWER OF SELF-VIEW

Most people think they're one fixed thing. This creates a problem. If you think you are fixed and bad, then you will be trapped. You will always think you are bad. Don't worry, though; you are neither fixed nor bad, as you will see below.

Let's see if you think of yourself as fixed. In the spaces below, respond to the following prompts:

Who are you? Complete this sentence:

I am...
_____

_____

Think about your answer. Does that describe *all* of you? Everything?

See if you can go one step further and describe yourself in a whole bunch of words. Create a "word painting" of yourself by completing the following sentences. Use an equal number of positive evaluations (great, awesome, strong, good enough, lovable, effective, good in English) and negative evaluations (mean, weak, not good enough, stupid, not lovable, bad in math). Mix them up across the page.

Your Self-Portrait in Words

I am _____   I am _____   I am _____

I am _____   I am _____   I am _____

I am ____   I am _____   I am _____

I am _____   I am _____   I am _____

I am _____   I am _____   I am _____

I am ____   I am _____   I am _____

I am _____   I am _____   I am _____

Now, as you look at the words you wrote, do you see *all* of yourself? We mean ALL.
Do any of these evaluations capture *all* of you? We mean ALL.

The answer is no. You could spend forever completing these "I am…" sentences and you would never run out of evaluations. This is because evaluations are just your advisor judging and making determinations. Your advisor can talk forever. Your advisor is just a part of you, not the whole you. And you hold the advisor the same way that your list of evaluations holds the words. You don't have to listen to any of these words if they don't help you. You can choose.

Self-view helps you recognize three important things.

1. Your thoughts (advisor) don't define you. You can have self-doubt and still succeed.
    For example, write a negative thought your advisor sometimes says to you.

_____

Now let's try a self-view switch. Say to yourself, *My advisor says to me* [insert negative thought above], *but I get to choose what happens next*. Self-view helps you create space between your advisor and you. In that space, you'll find freedom from worry and self-doubt.

2. Your feelings (noticer) don't define you. You can notice strong feelings and not react
    to them or be overwhelmed by them. Write how you're feeling at this moment.

_____

Now let's try a self-view shift. Say to yourself, *I noticed myself feeling* [insert feeling above].
I can hold this feeling and still do something fun or meaningful. My feelings are along for the ride. Self-view helps you create space between you and your feelings. In that space, you learn to pause and not react to your feelings. You'll find freedom from being at the mercy of your feelings.

3. Your past discoveries and mistakes (discoverer) don't define you. You can have regrets
    and feelings of embarrassment and still move forward in your life. In the space below,
    write about a time you made a mistake.

_____

_____

Now do a self-view shift. Say to yourself, *I made a mistake when I* [insert mistake from above]. *I know now mistakes are for learning. I can do something different next time*. Self-view helps you see that no single mistake ever defines you. You're not your mistakes. You'll find freedom to make mistakes and learn from them, and this will make you a better person, not a worse person.

Self-view is liberating because it lets you see that you're not fixed by your thoughts (A), feelings (N), or past actions (D). You can change your life and grow.

Anytime you feel life is horrible and will never change, just remember to get into self-view. Notice yourself as if from a distance. Remind yourself that things are always changing and you're always changing. Nothing you have thought, felt, or done in the past fixes your future. You choose. **Your life, your way**.

» THE POWER OF SOCIAL VIEW

We have one more viewpoint shift we can make, an important one. Just as Lee was able to switch from viewing himself diving to considering how others might see him as he dived, you can widen your view beyond self-view to include others, what we call social view.

This is the view that helps you get along with others, manage difficult people, build friendships, and find love. We will introduce you to social view briefly here, and then cover it in more detail in the chapters on building supportive relationships and managing bullies.

Let's start with a question. In the space below, respond to the following prompt:

What is most important to you?

_____

When people answer this question, they almost always think of friends and loved ones. Rarely do people say, "The most important thing is having an awesome car or being sexy." Those things might be important, but not *the* most important.

You're part of a social species called "human." You depend on other humans for everything. Think about it. You probably didn't make your clothes, generate the electricity running through your house, invent the medicine that makes you feel better, or grow the food you need to live. We're not lone individuals, but part of a tightly connected network. If people accept you, you'll feel joy; if people reject you, you'll feel pain.

You need social view to navigate social relationships. In the spaces below, respond to the following prompts to get into social view:

<u>Discoverer:</u> Think of someone you like. What does that person love to do? Imagine them doing that now. (Take 5 seconds.) Then write a few things down.

_____

_____

<u>Noticer:</u> What do you think they feel like when they're doing that activity? Try to imagine what it's like to be in that person's skin. (Take 5 seconds.) Then write a few things down.

_____

_____

_____

<u>Advisor:</u> What do you think their advisor might say to them as they do the thing they love? Would their advisor be different if they knew you were watching them and thinking about this? (Take 5 seconds.) Then write a few things down.

_____

_____

_____

When you use your **social view**, you're trying to see things from another person's perspective. You see that they have a noticer pointing out their strong feelings. They have a discoverer that can keep messing up. They have an advisor telling them what they need to do, or do better. And they have things and people they value.

When you take a social view, you can practice empathy and compassion for another person. You can learn to make friends and build relationships. Just like you, other people are constantly growing. You can use your social view skills to navigate your friendships, family relationships, and any relationship you care about.

CAN YOU GUESS WHAT THEY ARE DOING (D), FEELING AND SEEING (N), AND THINKING (A)? THAT'S SOCIAL VIEW.

YOUR LIFE YOUR WAY

» LET YOUR HEART GUIDE YOUR JOURNEY

Congratulations, you have completed DNA-V skill training. You have learned how to switch between discoverer, noticer, advisor, and self and social views. You've learned to consider your value and let that guide you. That seems like a lot, we know, but the rest of the book will give you opportunities to practice view-shifting. When you choose to do this, in the service of building value in your life, you'll be leading with your heart.

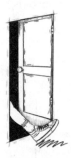

» EMBRACE CHANGE

In this chapter you learned that you're changing, with every thought, action, and feeling. This is great news, because it means you're not fixed. You can grow. You can improve.

» DEVELOP YOUR FLEXIBLE STRENGTH

In this chapter we introduced you to the self and social views. In the rest of this book you'll practice using these views to build value in your life.

» Self-view: You use this view when you see that you cannot be defined by your past mistakes (discoverer behavior). Nor can you be defined by your thoughts (advisor) or feelings (noticer). You are more than your DNA. You hold your DNA. When you recognize this, you become capable of changing and growing.

» Social view: You use this view when you try to understand that others also have a discoverer directing their behavior, a noticer with strong feelings, and an advisor telling them what to do. Social view will help you build strong relationships and manage bullies.

Your next step is to choose a chapter in the second part of the book to read. Don't forget, you don't have to read the book from start to finish. Focus on the chapters that are relevant to you. Now you're ready.

PART 2

FOCUSING YOUR SKILLS

LIKE A RIVER YOU ARE ALWAYS CHANGING, EVERY STEP IS DIFFERENT.

The ancient philosopher Heraclitus once said that you never step twice in the same river, because the river has already changed. And, having read part 1, you have already changed a little, even if you don't notice it yet. Hopefully, you're excited to move into the focused skills section.

As you move into practicing DNA-V in your life, you will be like that river, constantly flowing and changing to meet the challenges of life. And you'll become good at recognizing when you have stopped flowing, when you have become stuck.

Scan through the chapter titles in this section and dive into the place that suits you best.

CHAPTER 4

WHEN YOU CAN'T STOP THINKING OR WORRYING

Sometimes people use thought to not participate in life.

/ Stephen Chbosky, *The Perks of Being a Wallflower*

Why You Might Read This Chapter

Your mind never seems to stop.

You second-guess your actions.

You apologize all the time.

You overthink.

What You'll Learn

How to identify overthinking.

Why you can't just stop it.

Eight steps to DNA-V problem solving.

Five things to do when you're worrying.

Your advisor, or inner voice, is like a constant companion, walking next to you, always talking to you, trying to keep you safe, trying to keep you from making mistakes. You might walk down a hall and see a girl from your class and your advisor might say, "Don't trust her. She was gossiping about you." You might think about relaxing with a video game and your advisor might warn, "You'll get into trouble if you don't finish the math assignment on time."

Your advisor is essential when it gives you lifesaving advice, such as, "Don't cross those train tracks, it's dangerous," or "Don't eat that food, it's past the use-by date." Your advisor is so useful that you'll come to rely on it like a trusted and all-knowing friend. You might even believe it can help you with everything.

If something is stressing you out, you'll turn to your advisor for help. For example, let's say some person is making jokes about you and making you look bad in front of others. You might think, *Why is he treating me so badly?* You might ask yourself, *What did I do? Does he treat other people like that?* That's your advisor asking reasonable questions. No problem, right?

Except what if your advisor doesn't have an answer? What if you can't figure out why that person is treating you badly? You might spend an entire afternoon thinking, *Why me? What did I do? Is there something wrong with me?* You could lie in bed at night and still be thinking, *I should've said something sarcastic when he insulted me. But I'm too stupid for that.* The next morning, tired for lack of sleep, you might continue to ask your advisor, *Why me?*

The simple word for this activity is *overthinking*. If overthinking is impeding your life, you'll need courage to stop relying entirely on your advisor. Let go and move on. But letting go of the advisor feels like letting go of a safety shield and exposing yourself to danger; it isn't easy.

Letting go doesn't mean you eliminate worry or rumination. It means you learn to accept that your advisor doesn't have all the answers. It means you learn to move into the noticer or discoverer space, and connect with what you value.

» OVERTHINKING: VIRTUAL TRAVELING GONE WRONG

Everybody has an advisor that thinks in troublesome ways sometimes. When we're stuck listening to our advisor, it's like we're stuck in a virtual world, like these four young people at a concert. Their bodies are at the concert, but their minds are elsewhere.

See **Fiona** in the illustration, she had a fight with her friends this morning. Now she worries they will exclude her. The future has seized her. She feels butterflies in her stomach and wants to hide in the bathroom; she thinks she needs to get out of here.

Feeling isn't the problem. Fiona isn't being dramatic. She is stuck in "<u>future world.</u>"

Meanwhile, **Paul** is remembering something that happened two weeks ago. Paul was in the gym changing room, and they were laughing at him and calling him names. Tears came to his eyes. Should he have done something different? Hit back? Said something insulting?

Remembering isn't the problem. Paul isn't wrong. But if he can't shift his attention back to the concert, he will be stuck in "<u>past world.</u>"

Take a look at **Talia**. She is criticizing herself and seeing flaws in herself that aren't there. This isn't the past or future; it's like a "nowhere world." We all travel to this place sometimes and beat ourselves up. Here, Talia hates what she is wearing, she thinks she is fat, and she believes her eyes have ugly dark circles.

Self-evaluation isn't the problem. Talia isn't crazy. She is stuck in her thoughts of <u>self-worth</u>.

Now see **Rotim**. He is angry at his instructor for telling him to leave the class. He was sitting next to some guys who were talking, and the instructor got mad at him. Rotim is thinking about how the instructor hates him and is always unfair.

Evaluating others isn't a problem. Rotim isn't a bad person. He is stuck in his idea that <u>others are unfair</u>.

We can all do what Fiona, Paul, Talia and Rotim are doing. They're traveling to their advisor world. Their ability to travel to other virtual times and places isn't the problem; in fact, it's a superpower. The problem comes when they get stuck in a virtual world.

» WHAT'S YOUR OVERTHINKING HABIT?

What gets you stuck? Write the answers to the questions below.

1.   I get stuck dwelling on what happened in the past, about...

_____

_____

2.   I get stuck thinking about the future, regarding...

_____

_____

3.   I get stuck thinking about myself, worrying that I am...

_____

_____

4.   I get stuck thinking about others, worrying that...

_____

_____

» YOU CAN'T "JUST STOP IT"

When you worry, other people often say, "Just stop thinking about it." Have you tried to stop thinking about something and failed? Well, then, you're normal! There's a good reason you keep thinking, but to find out why, you need to play our "Just Stop It" game.

1. Pick up a pen and stick it behind your ear. Think about what it feels like, what it looks like, what others might think about you sitting there with a pen behind your ear like you're a star news reporter from 1942.

2. Now we will play the 20-point game. For the next 3 minutes, don't think about the pen. Every time you think about it, you lose 1 point. Your starting score is 20 points. Set a timer and gaze out the window or into space for 3 minutes. Get another pen and write an X in the space below each time you think about the pen. At the end of 3 minutes, add up your score.

Your X's   *Your score*

How successful were you at not thinking about the pen? People struggle to control thoughts, even for 3 minutes. This is because we don't have control over our thoughts. We can't make our advisor shut up. It's always on, always monitoring, always looking for danger.

Why? Because. Thinking. Is. Its. Job.

Even if you could avoid thinking about the pen for 3 minutes, odds are you couldn't keep doing it. It takes a lot of energy. Many things would remind you that you have a pen behind your ear.

Your advisor is there to think, to look out for danger, to keep you safe and to help you out with problems. You can't turn it off, because its purpose is to always watch out and keep you alive. So, we can't stop our thoughts, but we can train our advisor so we have other options.

There are paths out of the advisor world.

» **TRAVEL PLAN 1:** USE YOUR ADVISOR WHEN YOU HAVE A "FIXABLE" PROBLEM

The advisor is most likely to help you when you have some control over a problem. Answer these questions to see if your advisor might be useful.

»   A problem can be hypothetical (e.g., What if I never find love?). Or it can be real (e.g., someone is bullying you). Is your current problem real?   ○ Yes   ○ No

»   Is your problem likely to happen soon? ○ Yes ○ No

»   Do you have some control over it?   ○ Yes   ○ No

If you answered yes to one or more of these questions, then maybe it's useful to be in your advisor space and problem solve. Here, we'll explain a simple process you can follow to maximize the effectiveness of your advisor. Note that we don't just stay in advisor space when we do this. We also use discoverer and noticer. The discoverer, noticer, and advisor work best when they work together. On the next page, write your answers to the following questions.

Eight Steps to DNA-V Problem Solving

1. **Define the problem clearly**. (Be specific. "I can't get my studying done" is specific; "My life is a mess" is vague. Use I-statements to define the problem.)

   _____

   _____

   _____

2. **Use all of your DNA-V to approach the problem.** In this situation:

   I typically do this action (D):

   _____

   I typically think these things (A):

   _____

   I typically feel (N):

   _____

   I value (V) being a person who (write what kind of person you want to be here, not the outcome you want):

   _____

3. **Shift to noticer.** Take a few slow, deep breaths and center yourself. Feel yourself sitting there, in this moment. There's no rush. You can always use your noticer if you're unsure of what to do in a situation.

4. **Shift to discoverer.** Generate solutions you might try. Don't let your advisor talk you out of a solution by saying things like, "That's stupid" or "I'd never do that." Generate as many ideas as you can.

   _____

   _____

5.   <u>Shift to advisor.</u> Think about the advantages and disadvantages of each solution. Use the chart below:

Possible Solution	Advantages	Disadvantages

6.   <u>Now choose an action.</u> What do you want to try? How will this help build value?

_____

7.   <u>Notice what might result from this action.</u> Will it be hard to do? Will there be difficult feelings and thoughts? Most importantly, are you willing to make room for the difficult thoughts and feelings in order to take action?

»   **Yes** I'm willing to experience difficult thoughts and feeling to do the action (go to step 8).

»   **No** I'm not willing to feel distress to do this action (go back to step 6).

8.   <u>Take action.</u> Now that you're ready to commit to an action, it helps to use your advisor to anticipate problems. Think about what might impede your actions.

_____

_____

If [describe a possible barrier to this action], then I will [describe what you'll do if you encounter the barrier].

If: _____

Then I will: _____

» **TRAVEL PLAN 2:** ACCEPT AND EMBRACE YOUR ADVISOR

There are some problems that your advisor can't solve (for example, parents getting divorced, a health scare, regrets in the distant past). You'll know if you have one of these problems if you worry about something you have no control over. What can you do then? Remember, you can't turn off the advisor. Your advisor won't let you. But there are some things you can do.

» **Schedule a "worry session."** This is a 30-minute period in the day that you set aside to worry and do nothing else. It's like you're telling your advisor, "Let's get together and worry at 7.30 p.m. today." Your advisor will often be satisfied with that arrangement. If you don't set aside a time to worry, then your advisor will be restless, because it won't feel like it's doing its job of looking out for you. It will worry all the time. Pick a worry session at least three hours before your bedtime so it doesn't interfere with your sleep. Also, if possible, pick a specific and consistent worry time period and location each day.

» **Express yourself.** Write about a worry for 20 minutes. This isn't for problem solving; it's for self-expression. Write about your deepest thoughts and feelings in an almost stream-of-consciousness way. This process may not stop your worries, but it will prevent your worries from overwhelming you.

» **Build new advisor rules.** If a friend had your worries, what wise advice might you give them? See if you can give the same advice to yourself to make it easier for you to deal with whatever you're facing. It could be things like, "It's okay; this will pass" or "You can handle this if you just keep persisting" or "You can't change the past. Just do your best now." (Make sure the new rule isn't one that tries to shut up your advisor, though—you already found out that doesn't work.)

» **Get into the present moment.** Notice what is around you. You can do this anytime. Just take a few slow, deep breaths. Notice things you can see. Notice that you are here. Now. What will you *do*? Can you care for yourself, or do something fun, or discover something interesting? Do it, don't just think it!

» **Decide to step into value.** Consider the six ways to well-being (see chapter 1). Do a well-being activity and carry your worry with you.

» **Review the "accept" and "act" steps in chapter 2.** See if you can accept your worries and act anyway. If worries don't stop you from doing what you think is important, they quickly lose their power.

YOUR LIFE YOUR WAY

» LET YOUR HEART GUIDE YOUR JOURNEY

Here is perhaps the most important practice for you. Practice having your worries and still doing what is important to you. Don't let those worries stop you from acting. As long as you keep doing what you care about, your worries have no real power, and they will fade into the background like the sound of a radio in another room.

» EMBRACE CHANGE

We often need to change our relationship to our advisors. We act as if the advisor is in charge, but in fact we are the ones in charge. And we need to take charge. This does not mean shutting up the advisor. It means listening to the advisor when it is useful and not listening to it when it is not useful. The advisor does not have all the answers and cannot always protect us. Sometimes you'll need to let go of the advisor, just like you let go of a tool that has ceases to be useful. Get into your life. Then something new will happen.

» DEVELOP YOUR FLEXIBLE STRENGTH

For the next week, practice using your DNA-V skills when you overthink or worry:

» Discoverer: Be willing to carry your worries with you as you take risks and try new things. Don't let worry stop you from exploring life.

» Noticer: When you catch yourself overthinking, ground yourself in the present moment. For example, take five slow breaths and then notice five things around you (see the grounding exercises in chapter 2). Don't just stay fixed in your advisor space.

» Advisor: Use the DNA-V problem-solving process you learned earlier in this chapter if you believe the problem is fixable. If worry is not helping to fix things, then set aside time to worry (a worry session).

» Self-view: When you get stuck, remember: You're more than an advisor. You're the one who has an advisor, and you can switch to your noticer or discoverer, or consider what you value most. You can find your way forward.

» Social view: Do you feel alone with your worrying advisor, like you're trapped in a cave with it? Then invite someone else into the cave. Talk your worries through with a loved one. Your advisor may sing a different tune when it has to sing for others.

CHAPTER 5

WHEN YOU ARE ANXIOUS OR NERVOUS

Our fearlessness shall be our secret weapon.

/ John Green, *The Fault in Our Stars*

Why You Might Read This Chapter

You feel something bad is always about to happen.

You often sense danger.

You keep trying to control your feelings and thoughts, but it never seems to work for long.

You avoid doing things so you don't feel afraid.

What You'll Learn

Why anxiety is a normal part of modern life.

What anxiety looks like in your life.

How to let go of hopeless attempts to eliminate anxiety.

How a willingness to feel anxiety lets you do what is most important to you.

Anxiety?

You're there, aren't you, anxiety?

Oh yes, you're still there.

Thump, thump, thump, thump.

Damn. Here goes my heart racing again. I can't stand this.

Thump, thump, thump, thump.

Oh jeez. I need to sleep. I have a test tomorrow. If I can't sleep, I'll fail that test and then I'll flunk the class.

Thump, thump, thump, thump.

My heart won't slow down. Should I tell someone? This could be serious. What should I do?

Breathe. They always tell me to breathe.

Breathe.

Breathe.

Calm down right now!

Damn it. They always tell me to breathe, but it isn't working.

This is the sound of anxiety. When you're anxious, you're trapped in this game of thinking, feeling, and acting as if danger is always present. Your DNA-V skills can help get you out of anxiety's game; they become your secret weapon.

» WE LIVE IN AN ANXIETY-PROVOKING WORLD

We humans have many fears. Fears about ourselves, such as: *Am I too fat? Too unpopular? Too lazy?* Fears about our future: *Are my grades good enough? Will I get a job? Is there love out there somewhere?* And fears about the world: *Is the world getting too hot? Am I safe on the street?* There are so many responsibilities: school work, extracurricular activities, chores, a job. Plus, we wire ourselves into social media, which presents us with images and stories every day that elicit even more fears. No wonder we feel anxious.

Anxiety has become so common in modern cultures that about one in five young people report anxiety at a level that makes them feel so worried or stressed that they cannot sleep, study, or socialize. This means if you're in a classroom of twenty people, at least four of them are likely to have high levels of anxiety. Can you pick out the people with anxiety? Chances are you'd guess some right, but not all. Most people hide it pretty well. Maybe you're one of them.

So, what does anxiety look like? On the next page is a list of common things that can happen inside your body and mind when you're anxious, stressed, or worried. To help you understand them more fully, we've grouped them under noticer, advisor, and discoverer so you can see which of those skills you're getting stuck with and which skills you need to build up.

Noticer

What might go on in your body:

» Feelings of overwhelm

» Feelings of fear

» Numbness or tingling

» Dread

» Panic or heart racing

» Startling easily

» Shortness of breath

» Vomiting, nausea, or stomach pain

» Muscle tension and pain (for example, sore back or jaw)

» Sweating or shaking

» Feeling dizzy, lightheaded, or faint

» Feeling detached from your physical self or surroundings

» Trouble sleeping (difficulty falling or staying asleep, restless sleep)

Advisor

What you might think:

» Worry about lots of things

» Thoughts of disaster

» "I'm going crazy"

» "I can't control myself."

» "People are judging me"

» "I never should've said that"

» Worry about upsetting dreams

» Think repeatedly about choices you've made

» Difficulty concentrating

» Convince yourself you don't want to do something

» Think you have a physical problem, such as heart attack

» Think something is wrong with you

» Intrusive thoughts you can't block out

Discoverer

What you might do:

» Withdraw from social events

» Urge to do certain rituals to relieve anxiety (checking locks, doing things in a particular way)

» Avoid situations of uncertainty or fear

» Stay home to stay safe

» Avoid deciding

» Poor performance or grades

» Avoid important activities

» Seek medical advice when you're physically okay

» Excessively seek reassurance

» Compulsive use of Internet or social media

» TRYING TO AVOID ANXIETY

Anxiety symptoms are painful. It's natural to avoid them. But sometimes doing what is natural is not what's best. Take a moment to explore this idea further in the space below.

Do Anxiety-Avoidance Strategies Improve Your Life?

Take a moment to explore this idea further by checking your answers to the questions below.

Things you might have tried to stop anxiety:	Does it work in the long term (not just for a day or week)?	If you use this strategy, what is it likely to cost you?
» Drink too much or do drugs	○ No ○ Sometimes ○ Yes	_____
» Avoid all activities that make you anxious	○ No ○ Sometimes ○ Yes	_____
» Avoid people	○ No ○ Sometimes ○ Yes	_____
» Attack the person making you anxious	○ No ○ Sometimes ○ Yes	_____
» Play small so nobody notices you	○ No ○ Sometimes ○ Yes	_____
» Avoid confronting a bully	○ No ○ Sometimes ○ Yes	_____

→

»	Procrastinate	○ No ○ Sometimes ○ Yes	_____
»	Distract yourself with something (TV social media, gaming)	○ No ○ Sometimes ○ Yes	_____
»	Turn off all emotions	○ No ○ Sometimes ○ Yes	_____

Did you notice that many of the avoidance strategies cost you something you cared about? People skilled at using their discoverer, noticer, and advisor skills still experience anxiety, but they've learned something important: they experience anxiety because they care about things. They feel anxious about performing badly in a game because they want to perform well. They feel anxious about being rejected by someone because they want to connect with that person. Anything worth doing involves fear.

Would you be willing to let go of controlling your anxiety? Would you be willing to make your life about doing meaningful and fun things, rather than about stopping all anxiety?

Fighting with anxiety is like having a tug of war with a monster. The anxiety monster loves a tug of war, and the more you fight it, the more powerful it becomes. So what can you do if fighting won't work? You can let go of the rope. You can stop fighting and choose to be willing to experience feelings when doing so helps your life. Let's learn about willingness now.

Time to reclaim your values.

STRUGGLE OR LET GO.

» GET PLAYFUL WITH YOUR ADVISOR

A fun way to look at willingness is to play our game of "Would You Rather?" Consider the options below and put a checkmark for your preferences. There's no right or wrong answer. You can have fun by asking your friends to do the quiz too.

The "Would You Rather?" Quiz

Live at a wizard school		Live on a desert island	
Go out to an event and be surprised		Breathe like Darth Vader	
Know how you'll feel tomorrow		Be able to live in the moment	
Go on a dream vacation		Spend your days in your hometown	
Have mittens stuck on your hands forever		Drink nothing but black coffee forever	
Hang out with safe, predictable people		Be with someone who excites you	
Live cautiously and avoid mistakes		Live with surprise and wonder	
Have piercings		Have tattoos	
Make something disappear by erasing it		Dream something into life	
Be assertive		Be invisible	

Look again at the quiz and place a V next to any valued items. Some items are just there for fun; we don't expect any value in having mittens for hands versus drinking coffee. But there are other items that may hold value for you. Are there some items you value and so you chose that option, even if they may be a little scary to do? Or did you select items that make you feel safe and prevent you from getting anxious? If you chose something a bit scary, then we would say you're "willing to feel distress" in this situation.

Whatever you chose is fine. This game is just about learning how your anxiety influences you, and how you can choose to live with it. Choose to be willing to have anxiety so you can *have* value in your life.

» CHOOSE WILLINGNESS INSTEAD OF AVOIDANCE

What if you totally flipped your script? What if you willingly accepted discomfort and anxiety into your life, instead of trying to avoid it? That sounds crazy, right? Why would you accept *that*? Would you accept discomfort into your life if that meant you got more of what you wanted, not less—more friendship, love, and success, not less?

There's a key "willingness" question that you can ask yourself to flip the avoidance script. You can practice it now by thinking of the answer to this question:

> Am I *willing* to feel distress in order to
> [insert something important here, the thing
> you want, like work toward friendship,
> success, and living your life your way]:

> _____

> _____

> _____

If you said "yes, I'm willing," then you're already seeing what willingness can do for you. If you said no, it's okay; there's more to practice before you're ready. That alternative script goes something like this:

> I'm *unwilling* to feel distress, so I won't
> [insert something you don't want to do
> because it is too distressing]:

> _____

> _____

> _____

We can't always control how much anxiety we feel, but we do have some say over *why* we experience the anxiety. Whenever we face an anxiety-provoking activity, we can flip the script and ask ourselves this simple question: Am I willing to experience anxiety in order to do this valued activity? If the activity is important, we may say, "Yes, I'll do it." If it's not important, we may say, "No, this is too anxiety provoking for me. It's not worth it." Take the quiz on the next page to find when you're ready to flip the willingness switch.

Flip the Script to Yes

Action	Why might you do this? Is there value in you doing this?	How anxious would you feel if you did this: 0 (no anxiety) to 5 (extreme anxiety)?	Are you willing to experience the anxiety in order to engage in the action?
» Speak to a person you're attracted to	_____ _____	_____ _____	○ Yes ○ No
» Go to a party alone	_____ _____	_____ _____	○ Yes ○ No
» Compete in a high-pressure sporting event	_____ _____	_____ _____	○ Yes ○ No
» Present a talk in front of a large group of people	_____ _____	_____ _____	○ Yes ○ No

Now, list some of your own actions that might be anxiety provoking. Rate your level of anxiety and your willingness to experience anxiety.

» [Other action] _____	_____ _____	_____ _____	○ Yes ○ No
» [Other action] _____	_____ _____	_____ _____	○ Yes ○ No

The world is anxiety provoking. If you find yourself stuck in anxiety, the key is to keep moving toward what you value, with willingness, taking your anxiety with you. And if you get stuck, shift your use of discoverer, noticer, and advisor to see which skill works best.

Nobody can tell you when to say "yes" to willingness. There are no right answers here. You choose. We know one thing, though. Happy people say "yes" to some things. What will you say yes to today?

SOMETIMES WE HAVE TO BE WILLING TO EXPERIENCE DISTRESS TO GET TO SOMETHING BETTER.

YOUR LIFE YOUR WAY

» LET YOUR HEART GUIDE YOUR JOURNEY

It won't always be easy to take your anxiety with you. You may fall back into avoiding anxiety sometimes, and that's okay. But if you learn how to shift your viewpoint in your anxious moments to remind yourself of what you value and how you can get there, you'll be stronger, and your life will be better because of it. You'll be living the life you care about, instead of living the life of anxiety.

» EMBRACE CHANGE

We often need to change our relationship to anxiety. It's not the enemy. You feel anxiety when you care. Instead of fighting anxiety, you can willingly *choose* to feel anxiety to do something you care about. See if you can complete the weekly journal (on the next page). Record whenever you willingly allowed yourself to feel anxious in order to do something important. Remember, you don't have to do something big or super scary. You could choose something that elicits only a tiny bit of anxiety. Small actions can transform your life. Never underestimate the power of saying yes to willingness.

» DEVELOP YOUR FLEXIBLE STRENGTH

For the next week, practice switching your viewpoints when you find yourself avoiding something due to anxiety:

» **Discoverer:** Take a small step and do something you care about, and carry your anxiety with you.

» **Noticer:** If you notice feeling sick to your stomach, take a few slow deep breaths. Say, "I feel anxious. And, I can have this anxiety and move forward."

» **Advisor:** If your advisor torments you with worry, remind yourself: "My advisor's job is to look out for danger. It's not always helpful. Thank you, advisor, for those thoughts, but I'll keep moving forward."

» **Value:** Remind yourself: "I'm willing to have anxiety in order to do something I value."

» **Self-view:** Remind yourself: "I carry my anxiety, so I'm not just anxiety. Anxiety doesn't define who I am. My life is full of possibility."

» **Social view:** Remind yourself that others might be anxious too. It's hard to see from the outside. Practice seeing through the eyes of others (see chapter 6, "Inside-Outside Vision").

Weekly Journal

When were you willing to experience anxiety this week?

Action that was tough for me	What was the value behind the action?	How anxious did you feel: 0 (no anxiety) to 5 (extreme anxiety)?

BUILD STRONG, SUPPORTIVE RELATIONSHIPS

"But it does not seem that I can trust anyone," said Frodo. Sam looked at him unhappily. "It all depends on what you want," put in Merry. "You can trust us to stick with you through thick and thin—to the bitter end. And you can trust us to keep any secret of yours—closer than you keep it yourself. But you cannot trust us to let you face trouble alone, and go off without a word. We are your friends, Frodo."

/ <u>J.R.R. Tolkien,</u> *The Fellowship of the Ring*

Why You Might Read This Chapter

You struggle to connect with some people.

You're fighting with friends or family.

People have hurt you.

You struggle with the idea that friendship and love include the risk of getting hurt.

You fear being hurt.

What You'll Learn

What makes someone want to hang out with you.

What makes you want to hang out with someone.

How to use DNA-V to build relationships.

Discover your superpower: inside-outside vision.

Powerful friendship rules.

Let's start this chapter with a riddle: Guess the problem. If you have more of this problem, you'll have *less*...

Ability to plan and problem solve
Ability to sleep
Emotional satisfaction
Chance of living a long life

Did you guess that the problem was loneliness? Research shows that loneliness is as big a risk factor for death as smoking ten cigarettes a day or having a bad diet. We humans need each other. Literally. Relationships are like vitamins and minerals.

The hardest part of being human is that we need others, and yet this need also makes us afraid. Imagine you like someone a lot and you ask that person out on a date. Think of the extremes in emotion you would have if that other person says "yes" versus "no." It's like the difference between heaven and hell. The problem we all face is that there's no social connection without social fear. They're two sides of the same coin.

If we are to genuinely connect with people, we need to make space for the fear of getting hurt. We need to be willing to feel. This returns us to the willingness question we introduced in chapter 5. Think about this question for a moment:

<u>**Are you willing to feel the fear of rejection in order to experience the joy of connection?**</u>

Are you willing to take the life coin? Just as a regular coin has heads on one side and tails on the other, the coin of life has connection on one side and fear on the other. To take the coin, you must say yes to both.

Don't worry if you can't answer this question with a resounding "yes" just yet. You can work through this chapter and develop your DNA-V friendship skills. Because humans need connection, relationships are often the most common value we hold, so we will start with the center—value. What makes you valuable to others? What makes others valuable to you?

» WHAT MAKES A GOOD FRIEND?

Have you ever wondered what makes a friend for you? Each friend can be different, but real friends make you feel good about yourself, safe, and supported. Look at the list below and check which friendship characteristics are most important to you. Select your top five, and write them in the space below.

You can do this by yourself or share it with a friend. If you're completing this with a friend, select the characteristics you see and admire in them. Have fun and focus on each other instead of yourself.

Characteristics of a Good Friend

○ Trustworthy

○ Talks about interesting things

○ Fun

○ Popular

○ Likes sport

○ Listens to me

○ Makes me laugh or smile

○ Loyal

○ Good at telling stories

○ Is forgiving/doesn't hold a grudge

○ Is upbeat (often in a good mood)

○ Shares my interests

○ Smart

○ Attractive

○ Lets me know how they're feeling

○ Doesn't judge me

○ Helps me feel better about myself

○ Shows kindness

○ Supports me

○ Puts me in a good mood

○ Is creative

○ Is good at planning things out

Other characteristics:

_____

_____

_____

_____

Now review the friendship characteristics again. Which of them do you have?

What makes you a good friend? When you try to answer this question, notice what your advisor does. Does it get critical of you when you try to think of your positive characteristics? If so, that's normal. Remember your advisor's job is to keep you safe and prevent you from making social mistakes. It will search for problems inside you and find reasons you acted like a bad friend. It might say you're not attractive enough, smart enough, interesting enough, or funny enough.

Everybody's advisor finds problems to worry about when being with others. If only we could all see what others are thinking, we'd realize everybody worries and maybe we'd worry less. But we can't. Instead, we have to learn how to tune in to our advisor only when it's useful—that is, when it helps us build our connections.

So just ignore your critical advisor for now, and write five things that make you a good friend. You can use the list on the previous page to inspire you with ideas, or you can write things that aren't on the list.

Who Makes Up Your Circle of Connection?

Now that you've identified what makes a good friend, we will turn to your broader circle of relationships. In the diagram below, write the initials of your connections according to how close they are to you in your current social life. You can include friends, family, teachers, even pets. Put those that you trust and like closest to you. Put those you sometimes hang with, or occasionally come into contact with, further away.

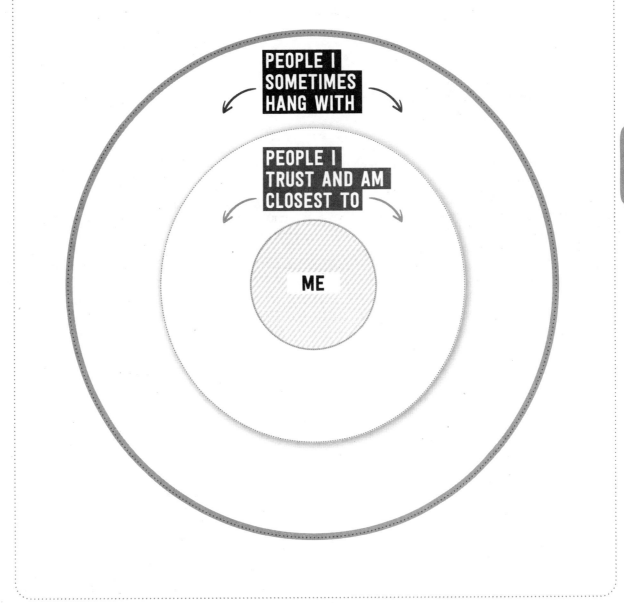

How do you feel about your social network? Are you happy with it? Are there any surprises? Are some people closer to you than you realized? More distant? Relationships change in surprising ways.

Do you see anybody with whom you would like to improve your relationship? Maybe you want to spend more time with them, have more fun with them, or argue less. Underline anybody you would like to be closer to.

Would you like to add new people to your social network? Maybe you'd like to change your social group, or build a new one. If you've decided you want to improve your social networks, the next two sections can help you think about how to do this.

» USE YOUR DNA-V SKILLS TO BUILD RELATIONSHIPS

Pick someone from the previous exercise that you want to be closer to. Do you ever argue with that person, or struggle to get along sometimes? If you are a human, rather than a robot, then the answer is yes. We would like you to think about this person, and the struggles you get into, as you shift through the DNA-V viewpoints below.

First, ground yourself with your noticer. Take a few slow, deep breaths. In any difficult social situation, pause and breathe. This will set you up to make the best choices.

Think of someone you want to be closer to. It might be a friend or parent or someone else. Think about a time this person upset you. Write what made you upset in the space below.

_____

_____

_____

_____

_____

Now take a walk around the DNA-V disk by answering the questions in each section. You can download a blank disk at: http://dnav.international. Or you can make a copy of the blank disk at the end of the book.

You can start anywhere in the DNA-V disk, but we find it's often best to complete the noticer (N) and advisor (A) questions first. Then complete the discoverer (D) and value (V) sections. Once you know your feelings (N) and thoughts (A), and make space for them, you may be more willing to try new things (D) to build value (V).

What difficult thoughts show up when you think about this person?

What behaviors have you been doing that make the relationship worse (lashing out, avoiding)?

What might you tell yourself that would help you build value?

What behaviors might make the relationship better (kindness, being open)?

What's important in the relationship?

How would you like to act to support the relationship?

What happens if you listen to different kinds of thoughts? Do they build the relationship up, or tear it down?

What new behaviors might build value?

What feelings and sensations show up in your body (anger, tension, resentment, sadness, fear that you will lose the friendship)?

Allow feelings to just be, instead of reacting to them. Take a few slow, deep breaths and create space inside you for the feelings to flow.

When you finish answering the questions in the DNA-V disk, you hopefully will be open to trying something new in the relationship, to build value. You might try having an honest conversation, asking how the other person feels, offering support, asserting yourself, or withdrawing from the relationship if it's too difficult right now. We don't know what's best in your particular situation, but if you engage in switching DNA-V skills, you'll discover what's best for you.

» BUILD SOCIAL VIEW: YOUR RELATIONSHIP SUPERPOWER

Relationships are confusing. One minute you're best friends with someone, the next minute they're angry with you and talking behind your back, and you don't understand what you did. People grow apart. Sometimes you find the friendship is a bad fit; perhaps the friend turns out to be immature or a bully. What can you do? A lot.

You can use social view to get some wise distance from the situation and discover what's the best next step. Social view involves you seeing how you're interacting with another person and also guessing what the other person is likely to feel, think, and do.

Let's start, as we often do in DNA-V, by grounding yourself in the noticer. You can do the following exercise any time, and it can take under 10 or 20 seconds (but remember, with noticer skill, there's no rush).

Outside-Inside Noticer

1. **Breathe:** Take a few slow, deep breaths.

2. **Notice outside:** Become aware of what is outside you. What sounds do you hear? Notice them, even the small ones. What five things do you see?

3. **Notice inside:** Scan your body from head to toe. Do you notice any sensations? Describe how you're feeling right now.

When you step into noticer space in this way, you don't overreact to your feelings or thoughts. You could feel angry with a friend but not seek to hurt them. You can feel afraid of what someone will say to you but not seek to avoid them. Your noticer gives you a strong foundation to stand on. **Remember this simple way to ground yourself with these three steps: <u>breathe, notice outside, notice inside.</u> That's it.**

Inside-Outside Vision

Now that you've grounded yourself inside and outside, you're ready to use your social view. This exercise involves viewing yourself in the relationship from the inside and outside. You also view the other person in this way. The table below captures the key steps. (If you want to do this exercise again, you can download the chart at http://dnav.international.)

View	You	Them
Inside	1. How did I think and feel? _____ _____	2. If I were the other person, how would I think and feel? _____ _____
Outside	3. How did I look on the outside? _____ _____	4. How did the other person look on the outside? _____ _____

1. When you think about the time you had a problem with your relationship, how did you feel? Were there feelings other than anger? Write them in the "Inside + You" quadrant.

2. Imagine you could step into your friend's body and think and feel what they think and feel. How might they have felt in the situation? Remember you're guessing here. You could be wrong. People cannot mind read as well as they think they can. The key is to imagine the situation from your friend's eyes and not just your own. So, take your best guess and write it in the "Inside + Them" quadrant.

3. Now, pause and consider how you might have looked to your friend on the outside. What would they have seen? Did you show anger? Or did you try to hide it and look cool, or unbothered, or even bored? Fill in the "Outside + You" quadrant.

4. Finally, how did the other person look on the outside? Did they look angry, cool, like they didn't care, or what? Fill in the "Outside + Them" quadrant.

Look at your answers. What did you learn from using social view for that problem situation?

INSIDE, OUTSIDE VIEW.

You probably discovered that your view of things from the outside is often not the same as your view from the inside. Often, what we see on the outside is not necessarily what's happening on the inside. Everybody hides what they're feeling. And usually we try to hide our insecurity and fear—and this means that just about everybody is looking more confident and unafraid than they're feeling on the inside.

To build strong relationships, we need to go beyond appearances; we need to understand what's going on inside ourselves and inside other people. But remember, when you try to understand what's going on inside someone else, it's just a guess. You shouldn't assume that you're right. Talk to them. You might have to change what you first assumed when you discover how they really feel. But odds are, if you try to understand what your friends are feeling on the inside—especially in a tough situation, like if you're having a fight— you'll be able to understand them better and respond to them better than if you were just going by what you see on the outside.

» FRIENDSHIP RULES OF THUMB

We call these "rules of thumb," because no friendship rule works every time. These rules often work, but not always. Remember to use your discoverer to test what's working for you. Here are some ideas that often help build strong relationships.

1. **Giving to others builds friendships.** Help others and support them. Do nice things without expecting anything.

2. **Good relationships are two-way streets.** Giving to others doesn't mean you should be a doormat—someone who lets other people use them. Remember, good relationships mean that the other person also gives to you sometimes and doesn't just talk about themselves all the time or use you.

3. **Wet blankets have fewer friends.** Look for ways to build your friendships. It's okay to be negative sometimes, but try to look for genuine ways to be positive in your relationships when you can. Your friends want to feel good about themselves and have fun. Look for genuine ways to build your relationships (coming up with fun things to do; paying someone a compliment when they deserve it; not complaining about every activity you do with a friend).

4. **Share wisely.** Learn the differences between sharing, oversharing, and undersharing. Oversharing occurs when you talk so much about yourself that the other person wants to escape you. Undersharing occurs when you don't let someone know anything about yourself; you remain hidden and distant. Both oversharing and undersharing are bad for friendships. It's important to share parts of your life, but there's a right amount. We can't say what that amount is because it

depends on each person in each situation. Use your discoverer skills to try different levels of sharing and see what works (go back to the discoverer section in chapter 2 if you need to check how to do this).

5. **Give friends your attention.** When others talk, do you make eye contact? Do you acknowledge what others are saying? People love when you make the effort to hear and see them. When someone is talking to you, put away electronic devices and give them your full attention. You'll make them feel great.

6. **Judgment and criticism are friendship poison.** People hate—and we mean hate— to feel judged. The quickest way to kill a friendship is to judge a person in a moral way when they may not deserve it (such as saying, "You're a bad person. You lied. You're untrustworthy"). Be careful about making these moral judgments. Are you using your social-view skills when you make them? If your judgment is too harsh or too fast, you'll get your friend's advisor going and they'll argue back. Initially, your friend's advisor might turn inward on themselves (for example, thinking, "I'm a bad person"), but it won't take long before they turn the advisor on you. Then they will use the advisor to attack you ("It's not me that's the bad person; it's you"). If something that a friend does upsets you, focus on their behavior ("I didn't like when you did that") rather than them as a person ("I think you're disloyal").

7. **Strengthen your willingness muscles.** Willingness means risking hurt sometimes in order to have a chance at connecting with other people. Willingness also means being able to walk away from a relationship when it has become too difficult.

8. **Be willing to apologize (but don't over apologize).** We all make mistakes in relationships. Are you willing to apologize in the service of building the relationship? A genuine apology can be one of the hardest things to do, but if you think you've hurt another person, we encourage you to apologize and see what happens next. You might be surprised. Your apology may release the tension in your relationship and make your friendship even stronger.

9. **Social view is your superpower.** Whenever you get stuck in a situation with a friend, or when you just want to be closer to someone, pause and practice taking a social view on the inside and outside of you and your friend. What do you guess they feel like? How do they appear on the outside? How do you feel on the inside and look on the outside?

10. **Social view isn't invincible.** People hide their feelings. Your friends are also likely to be struggling with things in life. Maybe they're experiencing a family breakdown, financial stress, a sibling who is sick, or a bully in their neighborhood. This is often invisible from the outside. You can always use your social-view skills to guess what's going on inside your friend when you want to be close to them, or when you sense they might need your support—but remember to stay open to your guess being wrong.

YOUR LIFE YOUR WAY

» LET YOUR HEART GUIDE YOUR JOURNEY

Return to your valued center often, reminding yourself what matters to you in relationships. When your advisor is being critical and making you want to lash out at your friend, pause and remember the list you made on what makes a good friend. Be that.

» EMBRACE CHANGE

Relationships change. They come together, and they sometimes fall apart. Embrace the change happening to you and your loved ones. This will give you the best chance at having relationships that are genuine and supportive.

» DEVELOP YOUR FLEXIBLE STRENGTH

For the next week, practice using your DNA-V skills when you want to build strong relationships:

» **Discoverer:** Discover new ways to strengthen your relationships. Maybe this could involve random acts of kindness, or just giving someone your full attention when you talk to them. Return to the exercises in this chapter and think of one or two things you'll try. Make a commitment—for example, a new social action you'll try.

» **Noticer:** Pause and decide whether you're willing to experience some strong feelings, maybe even distress, to do something new in your relationship. If you're willing, then try it.

» **Advisor:** The best way to commit to something new is to acknowledge both the potential benefits and the potential costs. This new action could be hard because... [try to think of the potential difficulties or costs for the behavior]. This new action could have benefits because... [try to think of how the behavior might improve your life and build value].

» **Self-view:** When you make a mistake in your relationships, practice showing yourself the same kindness that you would show a friend.

» **Social view:** Practice your inside-outside view. Remember that people often appear differently than they feel. Practice stepping into their shoes and seeing if you can connect by understanding them.

CHAPTER 7

MANAGE BULLIES

I allowed myself to be bullied because I was scared and didn't know how to defend myself. I was bullied until I prevented a new student from being bullied. By standing up for him, I learned to stand up for myself.

/ Jackie Chan, famous martial artist

Why You Might Read This Chapter

You aren't sure someone's behavior is bullying or not.

You keep getting bullied.

You often feel hurt by your friends.

You have trouble with bullying on social media.

What You'll Learn

What bullying is and is not.

What makes a bully hurt others.

How to take control with new skills.

How to work out a specific bullying problem.

In the last chapter, we showed that we need friendship and connection almost as much as we need food and shelter. That is why losing your social connections, or being bullied, is one of the most painful life experiences.

It turns out that humans regularly bully other humans. None of us, not even the bullies, escape from being bullied. For example, research suggests that over half of all youth have experienced verbal and/or social bullying in the last two months. Think about that. If you're sitting in a classroom with twenty others, about half of them have experienced bullying recently. Maybe you're one of them.

That doesn't make it okay. Even though being bullied is common, it's still painful. It doesn't mean we have to accept it or that we can't change it. It doesn't mean that we can't do things to discourage bullying. We can. In this chapter, you'll learn how.

» WHAT IS BULLYING?

Bullying involves two things:

1. **Aggression:** Someone is trying to harm you or hurt your feelings with their behavior.

2. **Repetition:** That person keeps doing it (it's not a one-time incident).

Bullying comes in several forms. They include:

» **Verbal Bullying:** Being called mean names; being made fun of or teased in a hurtful way; being called names based on race, religion, gender, or some other characteristic.

» **Physical bullying:** Hitting, kicking, pushing, shoving around; damaging your property.

» **Social bullying:** Being excluded; having rumors spread about you; having alliances created against you.

» **Cyberbullying:** Bullying using any form of electronic messages or pictures posted through any medium, including social media apps, chats, forums, websites, or email.

This includes trolling (constantly writing negative comments or disagreeing with anything you post), aligning people against you, or humiliating you.

» **Hidden bullying or narcissism:** This is tricky to spot, but it's when someone pretends to be nice to you one moment and in other moments they're being demanding or blaming you for not being a good enough friend. They make you feel bad for even small things you do, or expect you can read their minds and know what they want. It's like you never know what to expect from them.

It's important for you to distinguish between genuine bullying compared to behavior that's mean or insensitive, but is not bullying. For example, imagine a friend doesn't respond to a social media post, even after you drew their attention to it in a comment. Is this bullying? What about when someone you love is in a bad mood and says something mean to you? Or when you have a big emotional drama with someone because you like the same person, and they say hurtful things? Is this bullying? Here's how you find out.

1. **Aggression:** *Ask yourself, Is the person's intention to hurt or intimidate you?*

2. **Repetition:** *Ask yourself, Is it being done repeatedly?*

If your answer is no to both, then maybe the person made a genuine mistake. Maybe it's time to put some effort into the relationship, or maybe it's time to end it.

If your answer is yes to both, then it's bullying. Don't let it go. You can reduce it.

» WHY PEOPLE BULLY

Why are people mean to each other?

The most important answer to this question is that it isn't because of you. If you're getting bullied, it's never your fault. You have a right not to be attacked, teased, or excluded. You deserve respect. Everybody does.

Okay, so if it's not your fault, then why do bullies deliberately try to hurt other people?

» **Bullies need status and power—they need to be popular.** Bullies get something when they bully, at least in the short run. They get status and power. Imagine a bully who is scary and willing to hit someone or spread vicious rumors. You'd likely be afraid of that person. Maybe you would avoid them, or maybe you'd seek to be their ally so they won't attack you. Sometimes you might think they're funny or cool, as long as they aren't bullying you. It's usually easier to be aligned with the bully than against them.

What you may not know is that research shows bullies lose popularity over time; they don't keep their status for long. Why?

Even if you befriend a bully, it's only a matter of time before that bully turns their aggression on you. And when they do, they destroy your friendship, and the bully has to move on to someone else. Remind yourself of this; it may look like the bully is winning, but research shows they will eventually lose.

» **Bullies are often trying to make themselves feel good.** Bullying is like a drug. But like most drugs, it wears off and has negative consequences. Here are just some examples:

- Bullies may feel insecure about themselves—and they bully you and people like you because they're jealous of you. Attacking others makes them feel better in the short term. But in the long term, they're stuck with their jealousy and insecurity.

- Bullies might be angry about something else in their life and may take it out on you. For example, they might feel angry about their parents yelling at them all the time. This makes them feel powerless. So, they attack you to feel powerful. This doesn't work. Attacking you for no reason doesn't help them get any more power over their parents' yelling. But often, they feel it's the only thing they can do.

- Bullies may have grown up in traumatic circumstances where violence and aggression are what they've learned. For example, if bullies live in homes where people abuse, hit, or lash out every day, they may not have learned the benefits of being calm and kind.

Still, none of these situations excuses bullying. And none of these situations stop you from responding effectively to the bully. The first step to effective responding is to connect with your noticer.

Keep Your Feelings Real: A Noticer Exercise

You'll need courage for this exercise, because it's painful just to notice the difficult feelings that show up when someone seeks to hurt you or dominate you. Think about a time someone was being mean to you. Circle words from the following list that describe how you felt, and add your own.

Sick	Sad	Angry
Confused	Insecure	Unable to concentrate
Hopeless	Powerless	Unsafe
Afraid	Anxious	Resentful
_____	_____	_____
_____	_____	_____
_____	_____	_____

Remember, when you're using your noticer skill, you practice noticing your difficult feelings as they rise and fall.

You can then learn that you don't have to fight your feelings and that holding them in will only make the feelings stronger. It's like shaking up a bottle of champagne: eventually the cork will explode off (to remind yourself of this basic skill, see chapter 2). Feelings are signals in your body telling you it's time to do something. You can practice allowing your feelings to be what they are and choose a response that improves your life.

» HOW TO MANAGE BULLIES

There's no one way to handle every bully. It'd be great if we could get a bully to leave us alone just by being nice to them. But we know this strategy, like all strategies, will fail sometimes. This means we can't tell you just one or two specific strategies. Instead, we will show you a method for finding the right strategy among the many things you can try.

We will now introduce you to what we call the 2x2 PowerUp. This is a method you can use to find the best strategy to manage difficult people. We describe strategies along two dimensions. The first dimension is "self-power," or your power to be positive (level 2) or not be positive (level 1).

The second dimension is "social power," or your ability to interfere with the other person's behavior by either being assertive or attacking (level 2).

The 2x2 PowerUp Grid

Power strategy	Level 1 — Don't express social power	Level 2 — Express social power
Level 1 — Don't express self-power	**Ignore or escape the bully.** *Examples:* **Ignore:** Don't react to anything the bully says. Pretend not to hear the bully. Pretend that the bully doesn't bother you. **Escape:** Avoid the bully.	**Stand up for yourself or attack the bully.** *Examples:* **Assert yourself:** Say what you want or believe in a way not intended to hurt *them*. **Physically hurt:** Fight back or gang up. **Get help:** Ask an adult or others to help you.
Level 2 — Express self-power	**Be nice** *Examples:* **Be polite:** Stay slightly positive, but not overly friendly (you still have boundaries). **Be empathic:** Ask the person how they feel, or why they're acting badly toward you. **Be kind:** Include the person in activities, hoping it will reduce their bullying.	**Be nice and stand up for yourself** *Examples:* **Be polite and assertive:** "I'll hang out with a different group today.". **Be empathic and assertive:** "I see you're upset and think I was gossiping about you. I'm not." **Be kind and assertive:** "I'm happy to give you a second chance, because I like hanging out with you, but what you said hurt me. If you do that again, I won't hang out with you anymore."

As you look over these examples, how would you describe yourself? Do you mostly not express self-power or social power? Or do you sometimes express strong self-power and social power? Or a mix of the two?

Now you'll practice applying these strategies to a current situation in your life.

Use the 2x2 PowerUp Grid in Your Life

Think of a situation in which someone is bullying you, at least sometimes.
Pick a situation you want to change.

<u>Safety first:</u> There's an important advisor rule you should never ignore. Ask yourself, *Am I safe?* Pause and consider whether you're safe in this situation. If not, get to a safe place. Get immediate help from someone. You don't have to handle this on your own.

<u>Practice second:</u> If you're safe, use your DNA-V skills in any way that will help you learn to respond and reduce the bullying. Practice using your DNA-V skills:

» **Advisor:** What thoughts show up for you in the bullying situation? Write them below.

_____

_____

» **Noticer:** When you think about this situation, what feelings show up for you? Notice where feelings show up in your body. Write them down too.

_____

_____

» **Discoverer:** What's your old strategy? What have you been doing so far to deal with this difficult person? Has it been working? (Hint: If the bullying has continued, the strategy hasn't worked.)

_____

_____

» **Values:** What would you like to achieve? Perhaps you want to improve how well you care for yourself in this situation by getting the bully off your back. Perhaps you want to focus on your relationship with them and build that.

_____

_____

Discoverer: Now return to your discoverer. Try a new strategy. Use the blank 2x2 PowerUp grid to generate a bunch of strategies you can use to manage how you interact with this person. Don't worry about right or wrong answers for now. This is playful discovery. Make sure you include strategies in every quadrant. For blank forms you can print out, go to http://dnav.international.

Your 2x2 PowerUp Grid

		Level 1	Level 2
	Power strategy	**Don't express social power**	**Express social power**
Level 1	**Don't express self-power**	Ignore or escape ◯	Stand up for yourself or attack ◯
Level 2	**Express self-power**	Be nice ◯	Be nice and stand up for yourself ◯

Advisor: Now that you've written down the strategies, we want you to use your advisor to predict which one is most likely to work. Enter numbers in the circles from 1 to 10, with 1 being totally unlikely to work to 10 being extremely likely to work.

Noticer: Focus on what you think is your best potential strategy. When you think about putting that new strategy into play, what shows up in your body? For example, if you're thinking about asserting yourself, how does that feel? Tense, exciting, anxiety provoking, overwhelming, or something else?

_____

_____

_____

_____

Discoverer: Time to try that new thing. Which strategy would you like to try and discover whether it works? Are you willing to experience distress to do it?

_____

_____

_____

_____

Action: Take action. When will you use the strategy? What will you do if the strategy doesn't work? You can return to the power-up grid any time to review what you might try next or to generate more ideas.

_____

_____

_____

_____

» WORKABLE STRATEGIES DON'T ALWAYS FEEL GOOD

Okay, time to keep it real. We need to say that the most effective strategy may not be the most satisfying or the easiest. When someone tries to hurt you, naturally you want to retaliate. They're unfairly attacking you.

But a word of caution here: Aggression almost always backfires. When you hurt people or shame them, they don't just go away. They will think, and think, and think about how they can hurt you, and they will convince themselves that you're the bad person. Maybe they will gossip about you, or start fights with you, or try to get you in trouble with adults. Also, if you believe someone is attacking you and it's wrong, does it make it right for you to attack them back? What kind of person do you want to be? If you bully someone, you might find yourself more involved with that person, rather than less involved—and you might take part in the same hurtful behavior.

THE RELATIONSHIP TANGLE

TO UNTANGLE, TRY NEW THINGS.

YOUR LIFE YOUR WAY

» LET YOUR HEART GUIDE YOUR JOURNEY

When you feel sad because someone is hurting you, remember this is a message that you care. Self-care is just as important as caring about others. Connect with your values and practice actions that are caring of yourself first (see chapter 1).

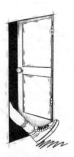

» EMBRACE CHANGE

Bullying happens. (It's still not okay!) Accept that the strategies you've used in the past may not work now. You may need to change what you're doing to manage the bully effectively. Try engaging your flexible strength.

» DEVELOP YOUR FLEXIBLE STRENGTH

For the next week, practice using your DNA-V skills when you're trying to manage a bully:

» **Discoverer:** Try something else. If you keep doing the same thing, you'll keep getting the same outcome. Try something new. Pay attention to what happens next. Did your new strategy work?

» **Noticer:** Engage your noticer. Pause, and notice how you feel around this person. Give it a label and a name. Do this, and you won't overreact to feelings of fear, insecurity, and anger.

» **Advisor:** Use your advisor to guide you.

  • Decide if it's intentional or repeated behavior from this person just to hurt you. If yes, then it's bullying. If no, go back to the friendships chapter and get some tips.

  • Don't blame yourself! You have a right to be treated well. Nobody deserves to be bullied.

→

- Recognize that the bullying may have hurt your confidence and well-being. Care for yourself. If you doubt yourself, work through the chapter on confidence. If the bullying has got you feeling sad, work through the chapter on sadness (chapter 8) or hurt (chapter 9). Whatever you do, take action. Trust that you have the strength to get through this.

- Take care online. Be careful how you respond to bullies on social media. When you're thinking about posting online, don't post unless you would want it to be on a highway billboard and left there forever for the entire world to see. For example, it might be a bad idea to take a photo of yourself giving the finger to a bully. Remember, your friends can view it over and over (and employers or future friends will look you up online). So, it's important to be careful about the things you post.

- Don't feed the troll. Minimize negative comments, posts, or gossip. Don't attack others online, even if you feel you're right. Don't retaliate. People will point to your attacks and make you look bad. You need to take the high road. We know that's hard, but it works in the long run. Block people online who are being unkind to you.

» **Self-view:** Remember, bullying is a problem with the bully, not with you. Don't be a victim. Practice with the 2x2 PowerUp grid to try different strategies and discover the best one.

» **Social view:** Get others involved. Talk to your loved ones to get support. Can you build an alliance with other people who will support you? Are there adults who can help? (You might be surprised by who will help.)

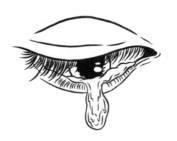

CHAPTER 8

WHEN YOU FEEL LOW OR SAD

The past can teach us, nurture us, but it cannot sustain us. The essence of life is change, and we must move ever forward or the soul will wither and die.

/ Susanna Kearsley, *Mariana*

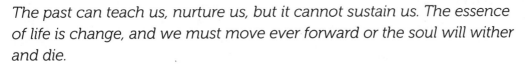

Why You Might Read This Chapter

You're trying hard to make sadness go away, but nothing you do works.

You're not engaging in many fun activities.

You're self-critical and feel worthless.

You try destructive things to punish yourself.

What You'll Learn

How to tell the difference between sadness and depression.

How to take the first steps to self-care.

How to practice switching from sadness to a life of energy and meaningful activities.

How to care about life in three easy steps.

How to use your discoverer to create new experiences.

Monday rolls around and your mom calls you to get out of bed and all you want to do is stay there—forever.

You drag yourself to school in a fog and your advisor is silent. It's not even helpful. Stupid mind. When your advisor does eventually get going, it's negative: *You're such a loser. Why are you even going to school? It's not like anyone wants you around.* You watch the other students at school and notice how happy they are; meanwhile, you feel nothing. The happier they are, the more you feel nothing. And then, "helpful" adults come along and tell you to just smile or do something fun. Stupid, aren't they? If only they knew what you felt, then they would just shut the fuck up and leave you in bed, in peace.

Ever have days like this?

This chapter is all about those times when your body and brain seem like they're stuck inside a bag of wet cement. Feeling hopeless. Sad. A stalled life. It happens a lot, to many of us, but sometimes it can feel like we're alone in our suffering.

» WHY YOU MIGHT FEEL DOWN

Sadness doesn't indicate that you're broken or have something wrong with you. Don't believe anybody if they tell you being sad is a sign of weakness. Rather, sadness is a message from your body, like a text message. It's neither good nor bad. Imagine you received a text message saying your best friend can't make it to the movie tonight. You might be sad, but you wouldn't think your phone was broken, would you? You wouldn't want to destroy your phone forever.

Sadness signals that something is going wrong. Perhaps someone in your life is treating you badly, or you're struggling with relationships. Maybe you're feeling uncertain about the future. Maybe you're not getting enough sleep. There can be so many reasons, and they can all pile on top of each other. Teenage years are a time of enormous change and uncertainty. Lots of teens, and adults too, feel low mood, or have feelings of worthlessness and hopelessness. If you feel low, know that you're not alone. You're a human with something to work out.

There are many sadness myths. If we believe them, we will spend a lot of time attacking ourselves for "being defective." Here are the most common myths.

» <u>If I feel low mood, I must have depression.</u> No. Some young people experience mood swings (but then, so do adults). Young people are passionate, which brings up and downs. Sometimes this doesn't feel good, but it's always normal.

» <u>If I'm sad a lot, there must be a chemical problem in my brain.</u> Not necessarily. That would be like saying that receiving a sad text messages means your phone has an electrical imbalance. Sadness is a signal, not a sign of disorder.

» <u>People tell me to "snap out of it." Are they correct?</u> No. Definitely not. Young people need support and can suffer more stress than at any other life stage. Every journey brings stress and mood changes.

» WHAT TO DO WHEN YOU ARE SAD

A word about depression before we move on. "Depression" is something longer lasting than low mood and effects all aspects of life—school, home, and relationships. Everything seems to lose meaning. About one in four young people are likely to experience depression during their youth. For most, it's a problem that occurs when there are major stressful events in their life. According to worldwide authorities, we should treat depression first with psychological and social support. This means changing the stressful situation, making schools safe, and helping youth develop supportive relationships at home and at school.

This chapter will help you if you're feeling sad or hopeless. If you're worried you might have depression, tell your family, and seek help from trained professionals. Here are some signs you might be depressed:

» Depression tends to be longer term than sadness (lasting longer than two weeks).

» You're not going out anymore.

» You're no longer doing your studies.

» You've withdrawn from close family and friends.

» You feel overwhelmed by emotion (for example, guilty, frustrated, irritable, sad, insecure).

» You're having thoughts like "I'm a failure" or "I'm worthless" or "Life's not worth living."

» You feel tired all the time.

» You think seriously of suicide.

If you have any concern about whether you're depressed, then we recommend you seek help. The research is clear on this. Seeking help will help you.

If you're sad or depressed, there's plenty you can do. So, if you feel like you're ready to help yourself, keep reading.

Begin with a Bit of Body-Keeping (Like Housekeeping Only with Your Body)

Have you ever noticed what it feels like to be in a place that's messed up and out of control? Like walking into a kitchen with dirty dishes piled up, the fridge full of old food, and mess everywhere, and you just stand there wondering how you'll get what you want.

Well, low mood is like this in your body. Your noticer is sending messages that things are getting messy. Here are five things that are a bit like housekeeping. Do these and you will help your body become strong and energized and your mind become more focused. No one wants to do them all, but they're necessary and they'll let some light in.

1. **Engage in physical movement.** Studies show that exercise has a powerful effect on mood, and some studies show it's more effective than antidepressants.

2. **Get enough sleep.** Did you know that poor sleep influences your ability to learn and remember? After just 16 hours of not sleeping, we start to become mentally impaired, like someone getting drunk. The greater the sleep deprivation, the more we will struggle to think well and act effectively.

3. **Improve your diet.** Do you eat a lot of junk food (soft drinks, fast food, energy drinks)? People who consume a lot of junk "fuel" tend

to be depressed. The type of energy you put into your body affects the kind of energy you experience during the day. Did you know that happiness and well-being improve with each extra serving of fruits and vegetables you eat in a given day (up to seven servings)?

4. <u>Practice your basic noticer skills.</u> Return to chapter 2 to review noticer skills and remember to use your breathing and mindfulness skills to get out of your stuck thoughts. See if you can notice the good things in your day-to-day life.

5. <u>Connect with others and give to others.</u> Return to chapter 1 and review the six ways to well-being. Try to do some of these small actions; they've been shown to help with sadness and depression.

Play the Random Switching Game

To play this game, choose one of these words:

<u>move</u>   or   <u>stay</u>.

Make it a random choice.

If you answered <u>move</u>, then follow the arrow and keep moving.

If you answered <u>stay</u>, you get to stay here.

STAY

MOVE

Welcome to the fixed space.

You can now occupy this space.

STAY STAY STAY STAY STAY   STAY STAY STAY STAY STAY

This is the place lots of people stay in while they wait for their "happy" feelings or thoughts to arrive.

Stay here as long as you want.

When you've had enough, choose "<u>move</u>" instead.

Now you've moved to here and you're free to go on to the next thing, whatever that is.

In these two choices, you've experienced what switching your DNA-V is like. It begins with a movement—even a small one, like scanning a page. You'll probably notice how much lighter it feels just to change that one small thing. Of course, changing real life is bigger, but it's the same action. Now you're going to practice doing this.

Rediscover Vitality and Value

When you feel sad, it's common to think your energy and joy have disappeared forever, but life is change, and it's good to remind yourself that low feelings will pass. Your first step is to switch to things you care about.

Think of things you love or that give you vitality (energy), even if just for a short time. Just imagine they're right in front of you now. You may have to dig deep, but allow the things you love to be in your mind now.

In the space below, write down at least four things that matter to you. Write a full sentence on each of them, including some of the details of why they matter to you. You can write about small, everyday things (music, coffee, blue sky) or big things (cooking with your nana, your last holiday). Here is one example to help you: *I love it when I can curl up with a good movie on my tablet, a cup of hot chocolate, and it's snowy outside.*

_____

_____

_____

_____

Now look at your vitality sentences. What does life seem like when you're focused on these? And now think about how stuck you feel when you're focused on hurt and pain. Can you feel a shift, no matter how tiny? If you're stuck inside difficulties, a small change of turning toward your values can be the beginning of bigger things. Remind yourself to connect to your values. You might even decide to do small actions right now.

Make New Advisor Rules

Now, you'll experience what it's like to switch into advisor space. When you're feeling low, this space can be very negative. You probably don't want to totally trust your advisor during these times. The good news is, you don't have to listen to your advisor. Remember, you're in charge, not your advisor (refer back to self-view, in chapter 3).

To illustrate this point, try doing these things only with your advisor—that is, only with your thoughts:

» Eat a block of chocolate.
» Dance in the living room.
» Throw snowballs.

How'd it go? Did you notice that your advisor can't do these things? Now, try doing these things:

» Tell yourself life is hard.
» Call yourself names.
» Consider the risk of trying.

These things your advisor can do. In fact, that's all you can do with your advisor—think, worry, plan, and predict. And because the primary job of the advisor is to look for danger and keep you safe, it often says things like, "It's too hard" and "You can't do it." Unfortunately, if you always listen to your advisor, you could end up hiding from life and doing nothing.

Practice flexibility by changing your advisor rules. You can use our new rules, or make up your own.

» The advisor's job is to look for problems, and my advisor sometimes makes mistakes with its predictions.

» Self-talk is helpful when it connects me to things I value. What are some other helpful things I can tell myself?

_____

_____

_____

_____

_____

» HOW TO CARE ABOUT LIFE RIGHT NOW

Now you're ready to switch to your discoverer and explore new ways of being. Remind yourself that you don't need to believe that things will improve; just say, "Yes I'll try something."

Try this discovery exercise.

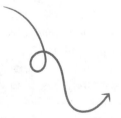

Discover Your Forgotten Joys

Step 1. Write five events that happened in the last few years. Don't worry if you're not sure what this means; just answer however it comes.

_____

_____

_____

_____

_____

Step 2. Now grab an electronic device (phone, tablet, computer) and spend a few minutes scrolling through any photos you've taken recently. (If you have no photos, spend a few moments looking at photos of places you like.) Just look over recent weeks, but don't go back more than that. Immerse yourself in the pictures for a few minutes and enjoy what you see. Imagine you are sharing them with a friend.

Now answer these questions:

» What happened to you as you looked over the images?

_____

_____

_____

_____

_____

_____

» Did you have images of small events that made you smile? What were they?

_____

_____

_____

_____

_____

» Did you have images of friends, family, and social life?

_____

_____

_____

_____

_____

» Did you have images of your passions, interests, and things you love to do?

_____

_____

_____

_____

_____

Step 3. Now compare step 1 and step 2. What do you see as the difference between step 1 and 2?

If you're like most people, in step 1 you would've called on your advisor to remember "important" events (note that we didn't say write "important" events). It's likely that the five events you wrote didn't include small things like the delicious ice cream you had yesterday, or the fun you had at the movies. That's okay, though; your advisor is doing its job.

Now, in step 2, it's likely that you used your discoverer. You didn't just think; you used your photos to show you things that you've done recently. Did you notice it was kind of fun to look at the things you've done? Maybe there were selfies or times with friends or family. Did you experience many small things like delicious ice cream or fun at the movies?

The contrast between steps 1 and 2 is important. Your advisor's job is to remember what might go wrong; your discoverer's job is to engage in experiences.

Now consider this question: Does using your experience help you move to something more vital?

PASSION GUIDES YOU

» **STRENGTHEN YOUR DISCOVERER AND LIGHTEN YOUR LOAD**

Now we invite you to go about your day and be curious. Your task is to notice whether some actions make it seem like you're dragging a heavy boulder up a hill, and whether other actions give you a lift, like you're released from the Earth's gravity. Then you get to choose: whether you want more granite (one of the heaviest rocks) in your life, or more helium (one of the lightest gases).

DRAG YOU DOWN

LIFT YOU UP

Granite: When you do these activities, they leave you feeling like you're dragging around a heavy boulder. Granite activities might involve calling yourself names, bingeing on junk food, or fighting with family members. If an activity feels like you've just put a heavy granite rock on your back and now have to carry it all day, then it's a granite activity.

Helium: These activities seem to lift you up; they put a spring in your step and make you feel like you can bounce along. These are activities like watching a funny show, texting a friend, sitting in the sunshine, listening to your favorite music, or doing something nice for someone else. If an activity makes you feel lighter, then it's a helium activity.

Activity Energy Meter

Fill in the chart to evaluate granite versus helium activities.

	Energy Meter (**before** activity)	Granite (heavy)	Helium (light)	Energy Meter (**after** activity)
	On a scale of 1 to 10, how are you feeling <u>before</u> you do it? (1 = I feel great 10 = I feel terrible)	When I do this, my day seems heavier.	When I do this, my day seems lighter.	On a scale of 1 to 10, how are you feeling <u>after</u> you do it? (1 = I feel great 10 = I feel terrible)
Sample List				
Listen to my favorite song	6 = A little lower than usual		✓	5 = I feel just okay
Criticize myself	5 = I feel okay	✗		9 = I feel really awful

Review your list of activities and consider all the things you can do that will lift you up. Consider writing a note of gratitude about one or two things that lifted you today. Remember that this is practice in becoming skilled at life. It isn't about never doing a "granite" activity; it's just about learning that you can change. You have the power to choose. And when you feel low, you can make the choice to help yourself, as best you can, until it passes.

Of course, we can't say what will give your life energy, joy, and meaning—things that will build your value. You must discover that yourself by trying things out and seeing what happens when a low mood hits.

YOUR LIFE YOUR WAY

» LET YOUR HEART GUIDE YOUR JOURNEY

Remember that no matter how sad you feel, in your heart is a light that shines on what you care about. Some people bury that light and end up in Zombieland. Not you. You have the courage to carry your emotions and choose a life of meaning.

» EMBRACE CHANGE

Choosing a meaningful life means that you'll struggle between changing and staying the same. Sometimes it'll seem like things don't change fast enough, and other times you may wish you could go back in time before change happened. Pause and breathe. You can do this. People overestimate how long sadness will last. Know that sadness, too, will pass (it still sucks).

» DEVELOP YOUR FLEXIBLE STRENGTH

For the next week, practice your flexible strength skills when you feel low.

» **Discoverer:** Practice the Activity Energy Meter exercise, increasing your awareness of which activities lift you up or drag you down. At the end of each day, write a note of gratitude for all the things that lifted you up.

» **Noticer:** When you have strong feelings, remember the basic grounding exercise, ACT, from chapter 2. Awareness of the breath (maybe take a few slow breaths). Center your awareness in your body and notice sensations there. Tell yourself how you are feeling. Take notice of five things you can see, hear, or touch.

  • Remember to practice the basic body-keeping steps we described earlier: sleep, food, and movement.

» **Advisor:** When you have critical self-talk, remember that you get to choose whether you listen to it. Pause. Remind yourself of new helpful rules: "My advisor is not always helpful. I choose when to listen to it."

→

» **Value:** Even when vitality and value seem a long way off, try to connect with one of the six ways to well-being (see chapters 1 and 2). Remind yourself that it's often the small things that bring joy.

» **Self-view:** Remind yourself that you're constantly changing. You're not just what your advisor tells you; you're also a discoverer, a noticer, and a person who values and cares about things. Choose to act in ways that allow you to see the bigger view.

» **Social view:** Connect with and give to others. The sooner you can reconnect with people, the sooner your sadness will pass.

CHAPTER 9

WHEN YOU HAVE BEEN HURT, BEEN AFRAID, OR FEEL UNSAFE

But I understood, now, that we don't live only for ourselves. We're connected by millions of shared experiences and dreams and nightmares, all tied together with compassion. I learned that even when we're going through our darkest winter, spring is waiting to appear.

/ Laura Anderson Kurk, *Glass Girl*

Why You Might Read This Chapter

You're afraid, hurt, or feel unsafe.

You keep thinking about things that have hurt you.

You feel strong feelings about past events.

You're mean to yourself because of past events.

What You'll Learn

Why you might get stuck.

How to respond to being hurt and grow stronger.

How to take a BOLD view to better deal with strong emotions.

How to practice self-compassion.

If you're in the middle of a dark experience, this chapter will help you nurture yourself and find a way to live your life.

It will help you bring some compassion and caring to yourself. But first, we'll consider the things that happen to people that leave them feeling hurt, afraid, or unsafe.

Bad things happen—too often. Here are things young people often face. Have these happened to you?

» Parents separating or leaving you

» Bullying

» Humiliation or embarrassment in a public setting

» Betrayal by somebody you trusted

» Being excluded by others

» Discrimination based on your age, gender expression, ethnicity, or physical appearance

» Neglect

» Chronic illness

» Bad accident

» Physical assault

» Tragedy in the family

» Death of someone close to you

» Sexual or physical abuse

Any of these events is likely to leave you feeling hurt, embarrassed, unsure of yourself, and even traumatized. If these experiences are happening, like many people you'll have strong emotions, feel unable to cope, lose sleep, get irritable or lash out, and feel wound up like a spring.

We want you to know you're not alone. Your experience is unique to you, but sadly, it's also common among humans. You can learn to equip yourself with the skills you need to manage these tough situations. You may doubt this, but research says the odds are on your side: you can lead a better life and live beyond your past, bad experiences. If you don't get support for these past experiences, you may blame yourself and beat yourself up. By reading this chapter, you've taken the first big step toward getting support. You'll learn how to release yourself from past hurt and grow.

Before we begin, we want to remind you of two very important points:

» It's not your fault if someone or something has hurt you.

» You can grow into the person you secretly hope to be.

There's something else we know from the data: all creatures, including humans, have adapted to survive even the toughest challenges. Animals who face risk and survive get stronger. Humans do too. Whenever you face hard times and get through it, you get a little bit stronger. Researchers even have a word for this: it's called post-traumatic growth. Post-traumatic growth happens when, despite adversity, you grow from that experience and use it to be stronger, wiser, and live a more valued life.

» WHY WE GET STUCK IN THESE EVENTS

When you face a threat, your DNA skills become hyper-ready to keep you safe. Your noticer and advisor are on alert to work out whether there's danger coming—sensing it and warning you about it. Your discoverer gives you ways of quickly reacting to the danger, such as lashing out at others, withdrawing to safety, or avoiding certain places or situations.

Let's compare humans to zebras. A zebra will run when danger is present and relax when it's gone. Not humans. Humans can stay in fight-or-flight mode even when danger is gone. We can do this because we can use our advisor to replay and relive bad experiences. A zebra can't get stuck thinking about the lion he saw yesterday 20 miles away on a different plain. In contrast, tough experiences leave humans ruminating and stressed. We want to turn off our stress system, and if our body won't let us, then we get angry at it: we cut it, or burn it, or drug it, trying to stop the pain. Still, no matter what we do, we can't turn it off completely.

There's an alternative. You can learn to use your DNA skills to protect yourself when needed, and to live with fun and vitality when not needed. Over time, you can learn that your feelings and thoughts aren't the enemy.

» GROWING YOUR COMPASSION

You'll now do a few experiments to see how you can grow from your toughest experiences.

Think about something embarrassing from your past, but choose an event that you now think is no big deal. For example:

» You mispronounced a word or used a meme incorrectly and people laughed.

» You wore the wrong clothes to an event.

» You said the wrong thing to someone.

» You put your hand up and answered a question incorrectly.

Pause now and recall a small mistake that other people noticed. Have you got one? Take a moment to relive that event again, imagining you're right back there.

» What happened inside your body at the time?

» Did you feel embarrassed, silly, small, or something else?

» What advice did you give yourself?

» Did you tell yourself you were an idiot, or worthless, or something equally mean?

» What action did you take? Did you remove yourself from the situation, mentally tune out, or something else?

» Did you say that you felt embarrassed or stupid?

» Did your advisor try to problem solve by telling you not to be so stupid again, like most people's advisor does?

» Did you then create a feeling of shame, so you wouldn't act so dumb again? Most people do that too.

The problem comes when you carry that feeling of shame into other parts of your life. Did you do that too? Did you stop making jokes, or stop putting your hand up? Did you avoid making all mistakes? That's the problem. A life without mistakes is a life without learning.

Let's try two steps to get unstuck.

Step 1. Ground Yourself with a BOLD View

Here is the foundation step that can help you reclaim your life. This is useful when the hurt or danger is in the past (if you're still being hurt, ask for help from a trusted person). Research shows that people who continue to avoid their own thoughts and feelings continue to experience pain, while people who open up to their inner selves, with a practice like the one that follows, can learn to carry their experiences and grow. This practice looks simple—so simple you might not think it works. Try it. It does. We call this practice "BOLD View." It is an alternative to the ACT noticer skill we taught you in chapter 2. Try it when you have difficult memories that make you feel scared, overwhelmed by emotion, or distressed.

» **Breathe:** Take a few slow, deep breaths. Your breath is the key to reclaiming your body.

» **Observe:** Notice any thoughts and feelings you're having in the moment.

» **Label:** Tell yourself what the thoughts and feelings are about. ("I'm thinking about the time they bullied me. I'm feeling embarrassed.")

» **Decide:** Choose your action based on what will help you become stronger and grow. Choose actions that will help you connect with vitality or build value in your life.

» **Viewpoint:** Remind yourself that you're more than this event. Take a bigger view and see all of yourself. Your memories and experiences are only part of you; you're more than this.

If you practice BOLD View when facing strong emotions, it can help you move on from the memory. You'll learn to carry the memory and live a great life. You'll need to practice BOLD View, but it will get easier.

Step 2. Practice Taking the View of a Friend

Think about what it feels like in your body to feel embarrassed or ashamed. Don't be afraid of these feelings. You are bigger than them. Let yourself feel. What is embarrassment like? Do any of these words capture it?

```
Weird    Ugly    Picked on
Defective  Worthless   Stupid
Awkward  Exposed  Regretful
```

Now imagine you see a friend feeling like this. How might they look? What might they say? Now consider your role here. What would you say to your embarrassed friend? How would you help them? Write what you would say below.

_____

_____

Now let's reverse it. Imagine someone who cares about you and wants the best for you—think of a friend or family member who you know wants the best for you. What would that person say to you about your embarrassing event? Write what they would say below.

_____

_____

Next time you feel hurt or experience something embarrassing, practice taking the friend's perspective. Speak to yourself like a friend. Try to extend yourself the same kindness that a friend would extend to you. (If this is hard because you're unkind to yourself, perhaps you can just start with moving the cruelty dial toward kindness just a bit. Remind yourself, "Sometimes others treat me badly. It's not my fault.")

BE A GOOD FRIEND TO YOURSELF.

Use Self-View to Increase Self-Compassion

This exercise will help you see your whole self in a bigger, healthier way. You'll see you're more than painful experiences. We will practice seeing all of you by completing the DNA-V disk again. See the disk here, or draw it, use the one in the back of the book, or download a copy of it from http://dnav.international.

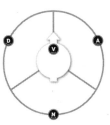

Advisor: In the advisor space, write some things you've used your advisor for by responding to the following prompts. It's okay to guess if you don't know the answer.

» A nice thing you said to yourself when you were little

» A nice thing you say to yourself now

» A math problem you could solve when you were four years old

» A math problem you can solve now

» A mean thing you might say to yourself when you're fifty

» A mean thing you say to yourself now

Noticer: In the noticer space, draw icons of things you can do with your noticer. It's okay to draw poorly or use stick figures—the idea is to use something other than words.

» How you feel when you're tired

» How you might feel when you're eighty years old

» Five things you love to look at now

» Five things you might love to look at when you're eighty

» How you look when you're sad now

» How you might look when you're twenty-five and feel sad

Discoverer: In the discoverer space, draw action stick figures. Just be playful. It isn't about doing it well; it's just about using something other than words.

» A movement you love to do now

» A movement you loved in third grade

» A movement you might love when you're twenty-five

» An action you did when you were in third grade and felt mad (such as yelling, hitting)

» An action you do when you're mad at yourself now (such as throwing something)

» An action you might do when you're twenty-five and mad at yourself

Value: In the center, write something you loved when you were four, something you loved when you were eight, something you love now, and something you might love when you're eighty.

Now, step back and look at the whole disk. Which parts of it are you? Notice you're all of these parts and that your DNA-V can change all the time. You're not your thoughts; they're part of you, and they change. You're not the bad feelings; they're part of you, and they change. Some parts seem to stay the same too, but you can always learn to do different things with them. For example, you react to sadness now differently than when you were four years old. Some values seem to stay, like loving others, but even the love we experience changes.

The point is, a person can grow and change. You're not the bad thing that happened. You're bigger than these things. Step back and take a larger view. You can learn how to use your DNA-V in ways that help you get the life you want.

YOUR LIFE YOUR WAY

» LET YOUR HEART GUIDE YOUR JOURNEY

If you've experienced hurt, fear, or felt unsafe in your life, remember, you're not to blame. You're not broken. You deserve fun and love, like all humans do. And you can learn to give love to others too. Keep having the courage to care about life and you'll journey beyond hurt.

» EMBRACE CHANGE

We block change when we don't let ourselves feel. If you try to block out hurt feelings, you'll likely get stuck in memories and struggle to move forward. Expect difficult experiences to make you feel stressed, on edge, and frightened. Remember that noticing fear and responding to it is a normal reaction and not a sign that there's something wrong with you. Let feelings come and go, and allow yourself to process the difficult experience.

» DEVELOP YOUR FLEXIBLE STRENGTH

For the next week, practice using all your DNA-V skills when you feel stuck in your memories or feelings of hurt:

» **DNA-V:** Practice BOLD View. **B**reathe a few times, slowly. **O**bserve your body sensations and feelings. **L**abel what is going on (for example, "I am feeling stressed out about this"). Decide your action based on what is important to you. **View** yourself as being bigger than the bad event. Say, "I am not this bad event." You can grow beyond it.

» **Self-view:** Practice seeing your life the way a compassionate friend would see it. Remind yourself that you deserve kindness.

» **Social view:** Try not to shut everybody out of your life. If you're continually distressed, seek professional help; you don't have to do all the work by yourself. With some experiences, it's tough to deal all on your own. Research is clear about seeking professional help: It works. Tell your parents, school counselor, or teacher—someone you trust—when you need help. You can't always avoid the bad stuff life throws at you, but you can do things to help yourself recover and grow stronger.

CHAPTER 10

WHEN YOUR LIFE ONLINE IS A HASSLE

I have looked in the mirror every morning and asked myself: 'If today were the last day of my life, would I want to do what I'm about to do today?' And whenever the answer has been 'No' for too many days in a row, I know I need to change something.

/ Steve Jobs, 2005 commencement speech, Stanford

Why You Might Read This Chapter

You spend a lot of time online.

You're not always enjoying your online time.

You feel disconnected from friends and need to check devices.

You get mad at games you play, or stuck on them.

What You'll Learn

How you're using online devices to build your life.

How online activities become habit.

What to do if you have lost time to devices.

How to change your online habits.

We're not your parents, so we won't be telling you to "get off that damn phone." We know you need to be online. That's how you hang out with others, game together, find out what's happening, have fun, and just stay in the loop.

Every generation of young people has had a hangout space. Before online life, young people hung out on the telephone. Often their parents yelled at them to "hang up the phone." And before that, in the 1970s, young people met at the local shop or café every day after school, and their parents told them to "get off the streets and get home." And before that, in the 1960s, they met at the drive-in, and their parents... We don't need to go on; you see the pattern. So first up, let's be clear: we know you need to hang out; it's how you share, learn, and grow.

This chapter will help you make some choices about your life online. Because we know that even though you need to connect, sometimes the online space can become toxic or a hassle. Technology can creep into your life in ways that you don't always want. This chapter is about how you can decide whether your life online is okay, and what to do if it isn't.

» IT'S ALWAYS A PERFECT DAY ON SOCIAL MEDIA

To be human is to experience both joy and sorrow, connection and loneliness. There's no being human without experiencing both good and bad. That's the reality of our lives. Social media does not present that reality. On apps like Instagram or Snapchat, you'll see people mostly having fun, achieving, and winning. Everybody's life looks awesome. What is the reality? People are not likely to post when they face personal hardship, so you are seeing a distorted, happy reality.

What happens to your DNA-V when you're online?

Your advisor will see all this winning and you'll have thoughts like, "Why is everybody doing better than me? Why are they out partying while I'm at home? Why do they have such a great life and I'm by myself watching television reruns?"

And then, when your advisor sees the selfies, "Why do they look so hot in their selfies when I look like a bear dragged me through the forest? Why don't I have a body like that?" Even if you're more into gaming than social media, it'll still happen. Your advisor might say, "Why do they keep getting the high scores and I get knocked out? What is my ranking?"

With your advisor comparing you to others like a crazed spammer, you might shift into noticer mode and detect some feelings of sadness and loneliness, or the dreaded fear of missing out. Then your discoverer might do some unhelpful actions—avoid real human contact, lash out, fight back, or something else. There is nothing wrong with you in this situation. You are just reacting naturally to the online environment.

Consider the image on the next page. How much are you influenced by the real world above the line versus the fake, pretty, shiny world of social media below the line?

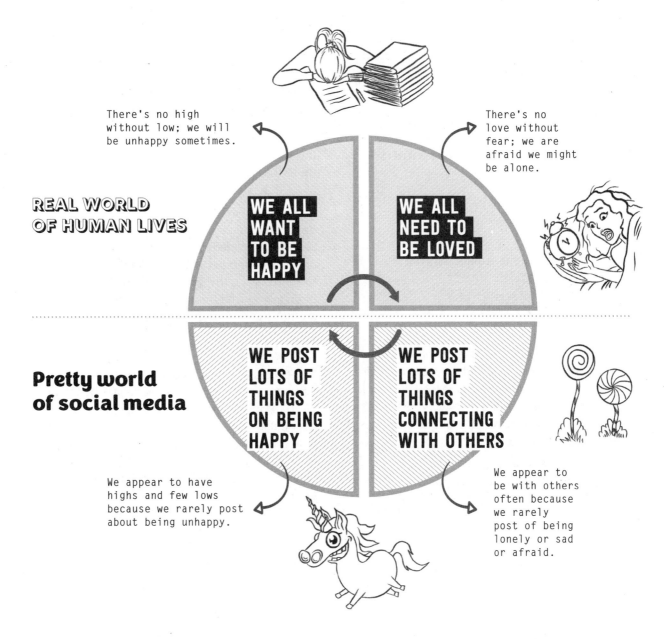

REAL WORLD OF HUMAN LIVES

There's no high without low; we will be unhappy sometimes.

WE ALL WANT TO BE HAPPY

There's no love without fear; we are afraid we might be alone.

WE ALL NEED TO BE LOVED

Pretty world of social media

WE POST LOTS OF THINGS ON BEING HAPPY

WE POST LOTS OF THINGS CONNECTING WITH OTHERS

We appear to have highs and few lows because we rarely post about being unhappy.

We appear to be with others often because we rarely post of being lonely or sad or afraid.

If we compare our life to what we see online, we will feel unhappy and lonely, because other people's lives look so much better than ours. The reality is, they look better because people rarely post the bad stuff.

We also act differently online than we do in the real world. Online, we rely on text or posed photos to communicate and we lose all the realness of our lives, the face-to-face empathy and kindness that we're capable of showing to real humans. Consider this: if a friend is standing in front of you crying, you wouldn't just tune them out and switch to another person in the room who looks happier, would you? You'd need to be a cold person to do that. Online, it's different. If you see someone in distress, you can quickly scroll up, or switch to another friend's page, and look at happy images again. Social media can foster avoidance of the messy lives we live. Real lives, as opposed to online lives, include low mood, anxiety, and sadness.

What can you do? You can use your DNA-V skills to act wisely online.

Whenever your advisor complains about how everyone else has it better than you, pause, and remind yourself of a new advisor rule for social media:

"It's always sunny online."

Remind yourself of those times when you've seen friends face-to-face and they tell you their life is pretty awful, and yet online their life looked mostly sunny and positive. Remind yourself of all those times you've kept things private, things that hurt too much to share.

When you post online, pause and remind yourself about your values. Ask yourself:

» "Does this help me to be the person I want to be?"

» "Would I say this if the person were standing in front of me?"

» "Does this bring me vitality and make me feel real and whole?"

» "Does this help me connect to the people I care about?"

When the answers are mostly yes (except for the odd rant—we all do that occasionally), you'll know you're using your online life to enhance your real life. Keep it up. If the answer is no, then it's time to change.

» WHY YOUR ELECTRONIC DEVICES GET YOU STUCK

Let's look at how online life trains you. Again, this isn't so we can tell you what to do about it; it's so that *you* can choose your life, your way.

We will start with some science. What if online sites—apps, games, and social media—are designed to grab and hold your attention and keep you engaged? That is, most online sites are designed to get you addicted. They want you to keep playing the game, returning to the app, or engaging with the social media page. If you do that, their designers are "successful," and they can charge you a fee, or advertise to you and sell you things.

So how did the creators of online sites learn to hook you in? It began with scientific experiments by B. F. Skinner, in which he learned how to manipulate and change behavior. He began with animals. He'd put a rat in a box and it could learn to press a lever and receive a pellet of food. If the rats were left to make their own choices, they would press the lever a lot; if each press gave them food, they would stop when they were full. Then Skinner discovered something important. If the rats pressed the lever and only got a pellet of food every now and then, randomly, it drove the rats crazy and they would press the lever continuously. They never stopped. They never had enough. Each lever press was filled with rat hope that the next time they *might* get a pellet.

Your online worlds use this science. You pick up your phone—oh, a message, great! Your social needs are satisfied, and you get a little feel-good buzz and a small hit of chemicals (dopamine) sent to your brain's pleasure center. It's like the hit you get from eating chocolate or some other addictive substance. Of course, you want that feel-good moment, so you check it again, and again, and again, and because it's random, you never know when you'll get the buzz, so you need to check *all the time*. Before too long you find you're checking your device constantly. When there's no message, your desire to check it increases. That's right—it increases. Eventually you find you're checking the phone all the time, from the moment you're awake until you're asleep. You might even sleep with it under your pillow and check it during the night too. That's when you know you're just like the rat.

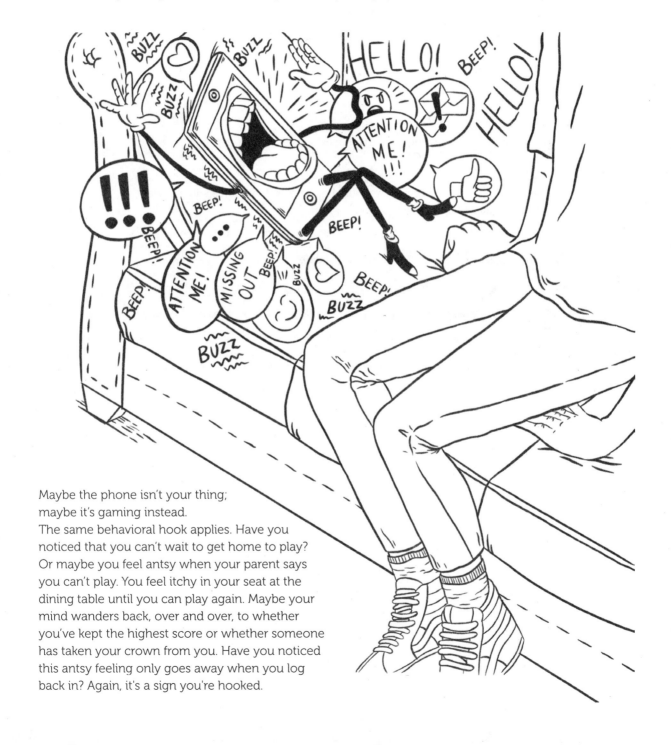

Maybe the phone isn't your thing; maybe it's gaming instead.
The same behavioral hook applies. Have you noticed that you can't wait to get home to play? Or maybe you feel antsy when your parent says you can't play. You feel itchy in your seat at the dining table until you can play again. Maybe your mind wanders back, over and over, to whether you've kept the highest score or whether someone has taken your crown from you. Have you noticed this antsy feeling only goes away when you log back in? Again, it's a sign you're hooked.

Here is a quick quiz to help you explore whether virtual life is taking over your life.

Quiz: Is Your Online Life Taking Over Your Real Life?

Check the statements that are relevant to you.

○ I can't stop. When I'm using an electronic device, I lose a lot of time.

○ I feel an urge to use my devices more and more, and it interferes with my life (such as sleep, family, friends).

○ Other people tell me I need to stop being online so often.

○ I get online as a way of escaping my negative feelings or personal problems.

○ I've lied to my family or someone else to conceal how much I'm on a device online.

○ I've lost opportunities because of my online usage (loss of relationship, job, grades).

If you agreed with one or more of the statements, it's a sign that your online life may be taking over. If you're ready for a change, read on. Your reward is balance. You can have both online and real life.

» TAKE BACK YOUR TIME

Deciding that you'd like to reduce your online behavior is a process that will take at least a few weeks. Just as the behavior of being online grew slowly, reducing the pull to be online will happen slowly.

First, let's use your DNA-V skills to take charge of your use. Consider the following questions and write your answers in the spaces provided. When you write out these answers, you're taking the first step toward strengthening yourself with some new plans for action.

Once you've answered the questions, take a screenshot and make this your screensaver. This will help you remember why you're choosing to change your online behavior. You have a lot to gain, but we often forget on an impulse.

What online or digital behavior would you like to reduce?

What will you gain by reducing this behavior (more time to do other, fun things; less feeling of envy; less tiredness; less self-criticism)?

What will you lose by reducing this behavior (missing out on important events; missing the latest gossip; being bored)?

What other meaningful things might you do with this time?

» TAKE CHARGE OF YOUR ONLINE HABITS

If you want to change your habits, you need to know what makes a habit. Every habit consists of three things: a cue, a routine, and an outcome. The following figure illustrates one "habit loop." In this example, you see your phone sitting on your desk. You're feeling bored and the phone reminds you that your friends are probably online right now. You mindlessly reach for the phone and jump on social media. In the short term, this is reinforcing. You feel less bored. However, long term you experience the anxiety of falling behind in your schoolwork.

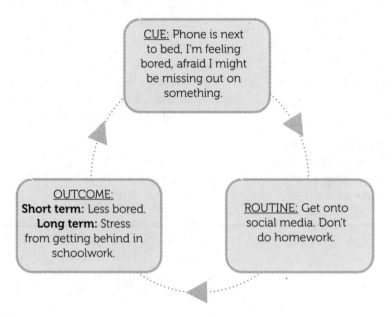

Breaking a habit requires you to change the cue and the routine. While you work through the following steps, think about the online or digital behavior you said you wanted to reduce in the previous section.

Step 1. Remove the Cue

Cues that link you to online behavior can be anything. They can be as simple as the image of your computer or phone, an alert from an app, boredom, or a desire to escape stressful aspects of your life.

Consider what usually cues you to engage online. What comes just before it? Does it usually happen at a particular time of day?

The easiest way to take away the power of a cue is to change your environment so the cue is less powerful. Here are a few ideas:

» Change the physical cue; for example, put your phone in the drawer instead of on your bedside table.

» Limit your time using the apps available to do this (there are many apps out there that can help manage screen time).

» Delete certain apps that really hook you or give you no joy (or change your notification settings to reduce notifications, so you can use your apps with intention).

How will you change your environment to make it easier to resist temptation?

_____

_____

_____

_____

_____

Step 2. Have Your Advisor Help You Manage the Cue

You can pair the cue with your own "online" rules. For example, you could have a rule that you stop using social media after 30 minutes, or that you don't get on social media before breakfast, after school, or when you're in bed getting ready to go to sleep. But, for the rule to work, you need to remind yourself of it. You can use a screen time limiter or a message on your screensaver to remind you of the rule.

What is your new online rule? How will you remember this rule?

_____

_____

_____

_____

_____

Step 3. Take Away the Cue's Power

You'll sometimes feel the urge to do your online or digital activity. There's no escaping electronics. But you can learn to react with choice to that urge. Here's how:

Shift into noticer and become an observer instead of a reactor. Start by noticing the urge to get online. What is your urge to go online? Say it out loud: "I have the urge to check Instagram." Don't act on the urge to hook into the online activity. Instead, just use your noticer to take a few slow, deep breaths. Just notice the urge without trying to control it or act on it. Be aware of any advisor thoughts, such as, "I'll miss out," "I've gotta play now," or "I need to increase my followers." Just take a slow breath and notice.

Now that you notice the urge, you get to make a choice. We call this the willingness choice. Are you willing or unwilling to change? (Note that there are no wrong answers!)

Do you want to do something else instead of the online activity? Ask yourself, are you willing to have this urge, and not react to it, in order to disconnect from the online activity and do something that you value?

If yes, then willingly accept your urge. Don't react to it. Move to step 4 for new routines.

If no, and you want to give in to the urge, that's fine too. You can go online. Do what works for you. This exercise is here to help you notice, pause, and then choose.

Step 4. Build New Routines

If you disconnect, what activity will you do instead? For example, we know that one reason you need your online life is that it helps you connect. If that's your reason for doing it, then it's best to replace that habit with a behavior that helps you satisfy this need. Answer these questions to help you build new routines:

» What does online life give you? If it's social connection, how can you get that? Talk to your friends about it; they might feel just like you. Maybe you can use video calling, instead of scrolling social media, or perhaps you can arrange another way to speak.

_____

_____

_____

_____

» Harness your noticer to become aware of when digital life is interfering with genuine friendship (e.g., you look at your phone rather than your friends). Write down some examples below.

_____

_____

_____

_____

» Is there something you value more than the online activity? It could be an offline activity, or another online activity that builds value in your life.

_____

_____

_____

_____

» Are there things you used to engage in that you don't do anymore? Perhaps it's time to revisit those activities.

_____

_____

_____

_____

» Use your discover to choose and track your changes. It's likely that you'll want to keep changing over and over until you get the online/real life balance right. What changes will you track?

_____

_____

_____

_____

YOUR LIFE YOUR WAY

» LET YOUR HEART GUIDE YOUR JOURNEY

Your online life is important, whether it's talking to others on social media or gaming. However, other things are important too: being active, noticing the moment, challenging yourself, and connecting face-to-face. Choose how you'll live your online life by considering what matters to you.

» EMBRACE CHANGE

We need to flexibly move between online and offline worlds. If you get stuck in either world, you're likely to lose something valuable. For example, people (often older) who refuse to use the Internet miss out on opportunities to connect with others and learn. In contrast, those who become addicted to online life, and can't seem to leave it, miss out on "live" relationships and school and work opportunities. Become skilled at changing between the virtual and the physical world.

» DEVELOP YOUR FLEXIBLE STRENGTH

For the next week, practice using your DNA-V skills when you want to make changes to your online life:

<u>Discoverer:</u> Here are three discoverer activities you might try.

1. Change up the cues to online use and see what happens. For example, "I put the phone in my drawer so I have to walk across the room to get it."

2. Create a new cue. For example, upload the screenshot of your answers to "Take Back Your Time" to remember why you're choosing to change your online behavior. Or write something encouraging on a post-it note and place it somewhere you often look.

3. Remind yourself of your new routines. Practice using your discoverer to try new things and test how they're working. Remember, you can always try something new if your current activity isn't working for you.

<u>Noticer:</u> Practice noticing and pausing. When you go to turn on the device, pause and consider whether this is really what you want to be doing right now. Notice. Pause. Choose.

Advisor: Remind yourself that life always looks sunny online, but real life has good, bad, and ugly. Watch out for your advisor comparing your life to someone's imaginary online life.

Self-view: If you find yourself hooked by something online, that does not mean there is something wrong with you. You are not an addict or broken. You are a human. The online world is designed to hook you. We all get hooked, and we can all unhook.

Social view: Social connection is like food for humans. We all need it, but some of it is healthy and some of it is junk food. Notice what aspects of your online world build genuine social connection and vitality. Notice what aspects are junk food—they are addictive but leave you feeling tired and nonvital in the long run (for example, spending an hour looking at random selfies). See if you can do more of the online activities that build genuine relationships (sharing, encouraging, being present to the lives of loved ones).

CHAPTER 11

DEVELOP AUTHENTIC SELF-CONFIDENCE

It takes courage to grow up and become who you really are.

/ E. E. Cummings

Why You Might Read This Chapter

You often feel insecure, and this interferes with what you want to do in life.

You resist taking risks because you feel insecure.

Your advisor beats you up with self-criticism.

You're waiting until you're confident before you try what you love.

What You'll Learn

Four steps to developing self-confidence.

How to bounce back from criticism.

How to keep doing what's important to you even when you're self-critical.

How to build your inner strengths.

How to have faith in yourself.

The central theme of this book is that change is the one constant. This is true for confidence too. You cannot stay confident all the time. You won't always feel good about yourself or your abilities. You'll fail sometimes, or life will throw something hard at you, and your confidence will drop.

Low confidence is not always a problem. Sometimes it tells you something useful. For example, if you don't feel confident enough to swim across a river, maybe you shouldn't try to swim across and risk your life (or at least have someone there to help you if you can't make it). If you feel low confidence about a test because you haven't studied for it, then maybe you should study for it.

Confidence only becomes a problem when it stays low and never rises. Then it becomes like a thermometer stuck at a certain level no matter how much the temperature changes. In real terms, if you find yourself stuck with low confidence, you won't be able to see opportunities. Then you won't try to meet new people, find love, or succeed. You just won't try.

In contrast, if you find yourself stuck with high confidence, you might become narcissistic. Narcissists' sense of their skill and importance is too high. They often talk endlessly about themselves and think everybody is admiring them. And they protect their high confidence by attacking others. So, you don't want high confidence all the time because you don't want to be narcissistic.

The confidence you want is not permanently high or low. Rather, it's buoyant, or like a buoy in the ocean. When the ocean is raging, the buoy sinks underwater sometimes, but it always rebounds up to the surface. It's almost unsinkable. That's the confidence you can develop.

YOUR CONFIDENCE CAN REBOUND LIKE A BUOY.

In this chapter you'll learn four steps to developing buoyant confidence. The first step relates to how we deal with the raging sea, or criticism.

» STEP 1: DON'T LET CRITICISM SINK YOU

To develop confidence, you need to first get in touch with criticism. Criticism seems like the enemy to confidence, but it doesn't have to be. Criticism is made up of words. It can elicit painful emotions, but no matter what, criticism is words; it can't control you. Let's get in touch with criticism now and see how you deal with it.

Noticer: Watch How Critical Words Affect Your Body

Notice the feelings in your body as you read the unhelpful advisor statements below. Even if you don't believe a statement, you might have some emotional reaction to it. Your task is to rate the intensity of the emotion you feel.

When I say this statement to myself	I feel this level of emotion				
	No emotion at all		Some emotion		An extreme amount of emotion
I'm stupid	1	2	3	4	5
I'm weird	1	2	3	4	5
I'm ugly	1	2	3	4	5
I'm fat	1	2	3	4	5
I'm unpopular	1	2	3	4	5
I'm bad	1	2	3	4	5
I'm disappointing	1	2	3	4	5
I'm weak	1	2	3	4	5
I'm not good enough	1	2	3	4	5

Which of these sentences elicited an emotional reaction in you? Do people say these words to you? Do you say them to yourself? Perhaps you sometimes hear these words in your head when you do poorly at something. They're painful even to read, aren't they? Criticism can feel like a knife in the side.

Advisor: Create New Rules for Criticism

Let's do a self-view experiment now to show you how you can change self-criticism. Get a blank piece of paper and write your most critical thought across it. Let's say it's "I'm not good enough." Look at this thought on the paper. Notice that you hold the thought in your hands—it doesn't hold you. You can choose to listen to your advisor or not listen to it, just as you can listen to or ignore lots of advice you give yourself. You're more than one thought.

Let's do something strange with your thought on that paper. Let's decorate it. You can do anything you want—color around it, draw cartoons to go with it, draw your advisor yelling it at you, whatever you want. If you have some art supplies or colored pens, you can use those, just to make it even weirder.

One thing we ask you to do is step aside from judgment just for now. As you decorate your thought, allow yourself to see what happens to it. Does the thought lose some of its power? Whatever happens is fine. **This is just about noticing thoughts and not reacting to them.**

» STEP 2: KEEP DOING WHAT YOU THINK IS IMPORTANT

WHEN YOU DOUBT YOURSELF KEEP MOVING FORWARD.

You can think of criticism as a zone, an area that you pass into and then pass out of again. When you find yourself in the criticism zone, you have two ways to respond. You can stop moving and stay there. This happens when you repeatedly beat yourself up with words. This also happens when you keep hanging out with people who often criticize you (you might want to read chapter 7 on bullying to help you with this).

If you don't want to be stuck, you can keep moving. You'll pass out of the criticism zone eventually, if you just keep doing things you care about. Maybe stop hanging out with critical people. You don't deserve to be criticized every day. Or, if you've experienced some failure, you can keep moving and doing what you care about. "Failure" is a thought in your head and a feeling in your body that will pass into nonexistence if you just keep moving. Sometimes you have to fake it 'til make it, so keep moving even if you don't feel you can.

The self-criticism zone feels real, like a prison, but it's really your advisor throwing unpleasant words at you. Critical thoughts are just sounds. They don't have to control how you act. The following exercise will help you see that.

Self-View: You Are Not the Criticism

The key to moving through the criticism zone is to recognize that the criticism doesn't define you. It's not you. It's just one space you go through sometimes. You don't have to fear it. Let's get into the zone now. Repeat the following sentence silently, each time with a different ending.

I'm bad at...

As you complete each sentence in your mind, make an X in the space below. Don't write the sentences themselves, just make an X for each time you complete the sentence "I'm bad at..." Do this for 1 minute (so set a timer now). Ready? Begin. (Complete the sentence "I am bad at..." in your head, make an X, and then repeat.)

Now get into noticer space. The Xs are there on the page, marking when you criticized yourself. Yet you're still here. You are seeing those thoughts. You notice the Xs. You're not the Xs, you're you sitting in the chair.

Do you see the spaces between the Xs? You're there too, in the spaces between the words. You're yourself the whole time. The criticism doesn't define you. You're more than words can say.

» STEP 3: RECOGNIZE YOUR UNIQUE STRENGTHS AND CAPABILITIES

We often feel like we *should* be someone different. Tall people wish they were shorter and not so noticeable; short people wish they were taller. Sprinters wish they had more endurance; endurance athletes wish they could sprint. Older people want to be younger, and younger people want to be older.

Let me (first author Joseph) tell you my story of trying to be someone else. I always wanted to be fast. I remember the day I discovered I was slow. I was lined up against all the people in my football team waiting for the race to start. The starter pistol fired, and I was off. I looked across the line and saw I was leading. Ten meters in, and I was leading! Then, something happened. People around me seemed to have a second gear and started speeding up and passing me. By the 50-meter line, a good part of the class had beaten me. I was crushed.

My slowness hurt me in many sports, such as soccer and football. I had a peculiar amount of leg strength that let me start fast, but didn't let me finish fast at 50 meters. You needed that 50-meter speed to excel at soccer and football. I always wished I was a different person. Faster.

But I kept using my discoverer and trying different sports. Eventually, I discovered where my specific skills fit—martial arts sparring. This form of sparring is light (you don't knock each other out) and fast. It requires speed at very short distances, about the length of a boxing ring. It was when I started sparring that I realized I could be fast, in this specific environment. Mind you, I'm not the world's greatest at sparring, but this sport suits my body type more than any other sport. I'd found a place where my unique set of strengths and skills fit.

The same will be true for you. You possess a unique set of skills, strengths, and capabilities that will fit perfectly somewhere. You may not know where or when that will happen. You may not know what your strengths are now, or what they might become. Remember, you're developing in unexpected ways. The key is to stay true to who you are and keep using your discoverer in new ways—test, try, fail, test again. Do that and your strengths will grow. Do that and you'll find your unique place in life.

Discoverer: Find Your Uniqueness

Read through the list below. Circle five things that are your strongest aspects or write new ones in the spaces below if yours are not shown here.

Drawing	Building things	Understanding other people's feelings
Taking photos	Talking with people	Persisting at hard things
Work as part of a team	Entertaining others	Exploring new ideas
Writing code/programing	Influencing others	Leading
Math	Learning new things	Running
Writing stories	Playing music	Lifting weights

Continued on next page

Playing sport

Writing essays

Asserting myself

Being open to new things

Organizing things

Caring for animals

Understanding my feelings

Taking care of others

Creating videos

Making delicious food

Helping others

Fixing things

Working outdoors

Mastering science

Selling things

Building a business

Being dedicated to others

Expressing myself artistically

Taking a systematic approach to things

Being physically active

Caring for children

Achieving goals

Beginning new things

Being in charge

Keeping my cool under pressure

Overcoming setbacks

Being brave

Understanding complex problems

Managing many things at the same time

Thinking deeply about things

Having a sense of humor

Planning things

Starting things right away, not procrastinating

Keeping my promises

Weighing the pros and cons of a situation

Cheering other people up

Having wisdom

Making careful choices

Being disciplined

Fitting into any social situation

Having faith

Being creative

Exploring the outdoors

Having hope

Working with cars or motorcycles

Singing

Working with my hands

Cooperating with others

Working with technology

Using social media to accomplish things (make friends, learn things)

_____

_____

_____

_____

_____

_____

_____

_____

_____

_____

_____

We will call these your five strengths. Even if you don't feel stronger than others at this, they are yours to have as strengths. The odds of another person having those exact five strengths is probably less than one in a hundred thousand, and in some cases, less than one in a million. Your particular combination of strengths makes you unique.

Now do some exploring. How might you use these strengths? You can have fun here—it doesn't mean you have to do it. For example, what kind of job might you do? What hobbies might you try? What kind of education might interest you? How might knowing this change your sense of yourself?

Now look over the strengths again. What strengths might you want to develop? Mark these with an X. You can build up any of these strengths.

Imagine if everybody in the whole world had the same strengths and weaknesses. We might have a world filled with football players and nothing else, or a world filled with accountants. That would be a disaster, wouldn't it? The world needs people good at different things, such as accounting, playing football, building, coding, dancing, writing, figuring things out, fixing things, and taking care of others. The world needs you to be your unique, one-of-a-kind self.

....

» STEP 4: ACCEPT YOURSELF ON FAITH

What's the difference between "believing in yourself" and "having faith in yourself"?

Belief needs evidence. Believing in yourself means you've convinced your critical advisor that you're good enough. That's tough to do, because sometimes your advisor will do what it has learned to do: be self-critical, for example. Even more important, your advisor has no delete button, so if you've experienced something, you can't forget it by wishing it away. You must learn to carry it instead.

Faith needs no evidence. Having faith in yourself means assuming that you're already good enough, even if it doesn't always feel that way. Faith is the key move. You can have faith in yourself even when your advisor is saying, "You have no chance" or "You can't do any better." Faith means having doubt but doing it anyway. So, your new advisor rule should be: <u>"I can have doubt and still take a leap of faith."</u>

YOUR LIFE YOUR WAY

» LET YOUR HEART GUIDE YOUR JOURNEY

Recognize that you're unique. You need not change. The world needs your particular set of strengths. Practice having faith in yourself. For instance, when your advisor says you can't, act as if you can. That's a faith move.

» EMBRACE CHANGE

There's no way to have permanently high or low confidence. Confidence, like all things, changes. Be like a buoy, which sometimes goes underwater in a storm, but always returns to the surface and never sinks. To develop unsinkable confidence, practice the following actions using your DNA-V skills. Remember, you can develop new strengths. You're changing. Become the change you want to see in yourself!

» DEVELOP YOUR FLEXIBLE STRENGTH

For the next week, practice using your DNA-V skills when you start doubting yourself:

<u>Discoverer:</u> Try new things to discover how you can excel. Confidence comes from doing, not from thinking.

<u>Noticer:</u> Notice when you're doubting yourself. What sensations show up when you feel insecure? Where are they in your body? These "insecure sensations" are only powerful when you don't notice them, when they stay hidden in the dark. Have courage. Acknowledge your insecure feelings. Bring them to the light and they will lose their power. Embracing your insecure thoughts is an act of confidence!

<u>Advisor:</u> What thoughts show up when you're insecure? Learn to recognize when self-criticism is happening. Try using the criticism to get better. Let it go when it's not helping you excel.

<u>Self-view:</u> When you notice yourself being hard on yourself, step into self-view. Imagine you're holding the criticism in your hands. Remind yourself: This is a thought. I'm bigger than it. I need not fight it.

<u>Social view:</u> When some people feel insecure, they try to build themselves up by putting others

down (see chapter 7 on bullying). There's even a meme for this: "Haters will be haters." You don't have to believe everybody's criticism. Know that people criticize or hate for reasons that have nothing to do with you. Use social view to understand why someone is criticizing you. Are they trying to help you? Or are they just trying to make themselves feel better?

CARRY YOUR DOUBT WITH YOU AND GO FOR IT.

CHAPTER 12

BECOME EXCELLENT
AT ANYTHING

And I wondered if hurdlers ever thought, you know, 'This would go faster if we just got rid of the hurdles'. / <u>John Green, *The Fault in Our Stars*</u>

Why You Might Read This Chapter

You want to be excellent at something.

You worry that something you want to achieve is too hard, or that you're not talented enough.

You're not sure how to improve.

You work constantly and feel exhausted, instead of excellent.

What You'll Learn

How getting in touch with values can help you.

How to see helpful stress and know unhelpful stress.

How the stress and rest cycle works.

The four barriers that slow your progress.

....

» YOUR VALUES POINT TOWARD YOUR PASSION

Confession time (this is Joseph, the first author). I hated school and didn't want to study or do homework. Other kids bullied me, the teachers mostly didn't like me, my parents didn't support me, and I couldn't see any reason to study. So, I flunked my English class and couldn't graduate.

I found myself at eighteen with no skills and no high school diploma, standing alone in the world. Where should I go? What kind of job could I get? I thought if I didn't get a high school diploma, I was screwed. I thought I'd have zero options in life.

That's when I realized that I needed to study, not because others made me, but because it would help me get a meaningful job. For the first time, I took ownership of my education. I went to summer school and redid my English course. Then, I entered the only university that would have me, one of the worst universities in the United States. I studied and, for the first time in my life, I started to get excellent grades. Not bad for a high school flunky.

What changed?

In high school, I went to school to avoid getting punished by adults. I was running from outside pressure. That changed when I realized what I valued. I said, "I want education. I need it for a better life." Then I started running toward a better future.

Can you see the difference? What does it feel like when you run from something bad? How does this compare to when you run toward something good?

So, the first key point of this chapter is this: Find your passion, the activity that gives you energy and purpose, and pursue it with all your life force. To do this, get in touch with your values.

Get in Touch with Your Values

In the spaces below, reflect on these two questions:

How will you strive for excellence?

Why is it important to you?

_____

_____

_____

_____

_____

_____

_____

_____

If you can find your personal answer to these questions, you will find your passion. Then, you will have the energy and focus you need to excel.

» DEALING WITH STRESS

The second part of the story, the part I (Joseph) haven't told you, is that school was hard for me. Going from bad to good is not like flipping a switch. I had to work hard and experience a lot of setbacks and failures. I wanted to be a writer. (Hey, I'm writing!) I took the right courses and studied and then I took an important test at the end of the year. I flunked it. Here I was, wanting to be a writer, and I'd flunked a writing test. (And remember, I'd flunked English in my senior year, too.) I started to doubt myself: Maybe I'm not smart enough to be a writer.

Studying was stressful for me. I had to work hard, and often felt confused and uncertain. I had to take on negative feedback from teachers and learn from my mistakes. Despite my doubts, despite my stress, I persisted. It took me ten years to get an undergraduate degree and a doctorate. Ten years! I had a lot of setbacks and failures during this time, but I didn't give up. This leads to the second key point of this chapter: <u>**There's no success without stress.**</u>

Notice Performance Stress

When you push yourself out of your comfort zone, what does it feel like? Do you feel stress? Do you feel focused, intense, worried, tense, or maybe all of these things? Think about what it feels like in your body. Write a description below.

_____

_____

_____

_____

_____

Strong feelings are normal when you push yourself out of your comfort zone. Such feelings let you know you're alive and you care. It's mostly good to be alive though, isn't it?

But Stress Is Bad, Right?

Many people will teach you that you should avoid stress. They even say you can live "stress free." Why, then, are you still experiencing stress? What's wrong with you?

Nothing. Stress is normal. The message society often gives us is the wrong one. Stress-free living is impossible. Imagine you're an athlete in the biggest game of the year. You want to win. Everybody is watching you. Do you think you can stop yourself from feeling stress? No chance. What if you're taking a big test and your future depends on it? Do you imagine you won't feel stress?

To become excellent at something, you must risk mistakes, failure, embarrassment, injury, and setbacks. There's no other path.

So, if people try to convince you that you can live without stress, just look at them like you would a snake-oil salesperson. Stress is not a switch you can turn off. Who is this person who leads a stress-free life, anyway? Stress-free people are dead.

Not all stress is good though. There's stress that comes from beating yourself up and having impossible expectations. That stress is not good.

Good stress helps you achieve excellence. Good stress occurs when you're challenging yourself with something that's difficult, but not so difficult that it overwhelms you. For example, if you're learning a new piece of music, you might pick something hard for you, but not something that's so hard that it's impossible for you to play. If you want to run a marathon and are out of shape, you wouldn't start day one of training by running 26 miles. No, you would run a distance that pushed you to get into better shape but didn't kill you.

Discover Helpful Stress

What is an activity that will help you build excellence? How might you take a step out of your comfort zone to get better at your activity? (For example, you could compete, or perform in front of others, or do whatever will encourage you to step out of your comfort zone toward better performance.) Make a list of actions you can take below.

_____

_____

_____

_____

_____

Stress and Rest

It's pretty clear you need some stress if you'll achieve your best performance. But stress is not enough. There's one more ingredient that's essential to success. Can you guess what it is?

Rest.

You won't improve if you don't recover from the stress. When you're building muscle, you need to rest your muscles (usually a full day). If you're doing something mentally taxing, you need to take regular breaks (usually about 10 minutes). Relax, let go, and recharge. If you don't, your performance will diminish.

The following image shows the typical cycle you need to go through to achieve peak performance. You begin by working hard at something and exposing yourself to discomfort, mistakes, fatigue, muscle soreness, failure, self-doubt, and who knows what other unpleasant stuff.

After you've put yourself under stress, you need to allow your mind and body to rejuvenate. Rest is not wasting time. It's a central stone in the path to excellence. So, you don't have to feel guilty about resting. It's good for you and it's what you need to reach your full potential.

Discover Helpful Rest

In this exercise, you'll learn more about the stress-rest cycle and how to identify meaningful forms of rest. Write the answers to the following questions in the spaces below.

1. **Identify something in your discomfort zone.** It could be studying, training, playing sport, playing an instrument, whatever you want. The point is, you're doing something that stresses your mind or body.

   _____

   _____

2. **Try different stress and rest intervals.** See what works for you. For example, if you're studying, you might try 25 minutes of work, and 5 or 10 minutes of rest. Or maybe you can go a lot longer than that—say, 50 minutes work and 10 minutes of rest. What new stress-rest interval would you like to try?

   _____

   _____

3. **Try different types of rest.** How do you best switch off? Maybe it's a 20-minute nap, reading a book, taking a quick walk, stretching, watching YouTube videos, listening to music, talking to a friend, scrolling social media, taking a shower, or getting into nature. What types of rest would you like to try?

   _____

   _____

4. **Pay attention to what happens next.** Evaluate which stress-rest cycle works best for you. Does it depend on what you're doing (physical activity versus studying)? What types of rest are most rejuvenating for you?

   _____

   _____

··

» THE FOUR BARRIERS TO BECOMING EXCELLENT

Now that you've learned the basics on how to become excellent at anything—good stress plus rest—let's anticipate a few things that might impede you achieving success.

Barrier 1: Doing Too Much Work

Stress without rest will worsen your performance. If you stress your muscles too much, you'll grow weaker. If you stress your mind too much, you'll feel fatigued, confused, and unable to learn. Doing too much work may also kill your motivation.

<u>Do you feel any of the following when you overwork?</u>

Burnout

Constant pressure

Feeling stuck

Feeling overwhelmed

Tiredness

Feeling tense and irritable

Let your body be an early warning system. Notice feelings of overwhelm, see them rising in your body, and take action to reduce them. Get more rest. If you can, reset your goals (focus on something you care about and have energy for).

Barrier 2: Doing the Wrong Kind of Work

Everybody knows you need to work to improve. You don't get better just by lying on your back and looking at the clouds (unless you're in your rest phase). But practice is not enough. For example, your parents might have practiced driving a car for years and years, but do you think they could drive a race car? Probably not. Routine work doesn't make you excellent.

The key to improvement is called "deliberate practice." Deliberate practice involves an intense focus on mastering a specific goal. Let's take a quick look at different areas of excellence and see what deliberate practice looks like.

- Nic Lamb, a famous surfer, says that during training, he tries to ride waves that scare him, so he can challenge himself to practice.

- Students who struggle on hard problems but work to figure them out do better than those who receive support from a teacher before they have a chance to try it for themselves.

- Ordinary violinists and great violinists practice the same amount of time, but great violinists spend more time intensely focused on mastering specific goals.

- Amateur and professional singers practice in different ways. When amateurs sing, they increasingly relax and feel positive. When professionals sing, they become more focused and aroused—but they don't feel more positive.

We can see why few people become excellent. It's hard. You feel fatigue, stress, and failure. It's not always fun. But if you can push yourself out of your comfort zone, and regularly engage in deliberate practice, you'll achieve excellence.

Barrier 3: Procrastination

Society often sends you the message that you should avoid stress. We have argued that you need to embrace stress to become excellent. Those are two incompatible ideas. They cannot exist together. When the societal message "avoid stress" wins the day, we procrastinate—we put off our journey to excellence. Weight lifters are notorious for avoiding the most stressful leg workout days. Martial artists often avoid training their nondominant side, because they aren't as good at kicking on that side. Piano players put off practicing a difficult piece. Football players put off running those agonizing sprints. And students put off studying.

Procrastination is a way of avoiding stress. But does it work? When you put something off, you feel okay in the short term. Maybe you procrastinate by watching your favorite show or playing a video game or interacting on social media and you feel okay then. But the task you've put off always comes back to you. The homework is still due. The sprints still need to be run. And then you feel more stressed because you're falling behind. What if, instead, you chose to make a small, manageable start?

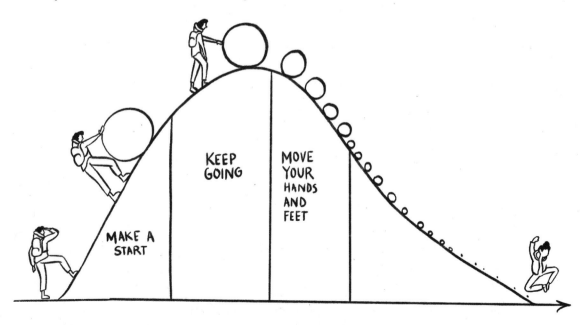

To minimize procrastination, try the following:

1. Choose a small step to start with. A huge step would be "become a leading app developer." A small step would be "study app design for 10 minutes each day."

2. Pick a time to practice. Be specific. Link it to a routine. For example, "I'll do my 10 minutes of research on app design after dinner."

3. Set a goal to do this for three days. Congratulate yourself for doing it.

Then after three days, decide whether you want to set another goal or change as needed.

Can you do something difficult for three days? Most of us procrastinate because we set goals that are so far out of our reach that we feel overwhelmed. To begin anything, start with small, meaningful steps.

Barrier 4: Listening to Your Critical Advisor

Last, we come to the barrier inside of us. Whenever we want to learn a new thing or step out of our comfort zone, our advisor may tell us to stop. Remember, your advisor is like a problem-finding machine, a machine you can never turn off. Maybe your advisor says to you, "It's too hard, you're not smart enough" or "This will take too long, you'll never get there" or "This is uncomfortable, stop now." The advisor is trying to protect you and avoid failure.

You don't have to make your advisor say positive things. You just have to learn to live with your advisor. When you push yourself out of your comfort zone, know that your advisor will spot problems and say you won't succeed. Everybody's advisor does this. Next time you step out of your comfort zone and your advisor criticizes you, you might just say, "Thanks advisor, but I got this. I'm going for excellence."

YOUR LIFE YOUR WAY

» LET YOUR HEART GUIDE YOUR JOURNEY

Why do you strive? Do you strive only to please others? Then you're unlikely to sustain your motivation during the tough times. Do you strive only because you want to beat others? Then you'll avoid losing and you will, ironically, not get better. Instead of focusing on pleasing others or beating others, focus on why you love challenging yourself. Remember what it feels like to improve. Do you feel joy? Satisfaction? Pride? Remember why you love performing at a high level. Let your love be the reason for your journey to excellence.

» EMBRACE CHANGE

Don't expect to feel inspired during the entire journey toward excellence. The journey is not just stressful; it's long, repetitive, and often boring. Expect your motivation level to change. An athlete practices the same motion for years; a musician practices the same pieces of music hundreds of times. Even professional video game players get bored practicing the game sometimes, but the best of them still practice. Recognize that during the journey to excellence, you'll feel motivated, unmotivated, excited, stressed, confident, insecure, inspired, and angry. Embrace all these changes and stay on your journey.

» DEVELOP YOUR FLEXIBLE STRENGTH

For the next week, practice using your DNA-V skills when you question whether pursuing excellence is a worthy goal:

<u>Values:</u> Remind yourself that you value excellence. "I value getting better at…".

<u>Discoverer:</u> Choose your steps toward action. Try new ways to push yourself out of your comfort zone. Try new ways to rest and recover. Say to yourself, "To get better, I will…"

Continued on next page

Noticer: Be aware of how your body is feeling. Notice when you're burning out or feeling unusually fatigued. You may need to rest.

Advisor: Plan your journey to excellence with some rules of thumb:

1. If I'm overworking, I'll rest.

2. If I'm doing the wrong kind of work, I'll focus on deliberate practice.

3. If I'm procrastinating, I'll break my problem into small steps and set a time to take that first step.

4. If my advisor is discouraging me, I'll get into discoverer mode and do something new anyway. My advisor will learn from my new actions.

Self-view: Your advisor is sometimes pessimistic about how much you can improve. Don't believe the hype! Your advisor is often wrong. People can improve far more than they think. Research shows that practicing something can cause deep changes in your body and brain. For example, practicing something in a new way increases the amount of white matter (good stuff) in your brain. Remember, you're not static. Who knows how excellent you can become (certainly not your advisor)?

Social view: When you strive for excellence, you're often competing with others. Maybe you're trying to make the starting lineup on a team, or be in the first position in dance or the orchestra. Maybe you're trying to get top marks in a course or design a better business than others. Competition can create tension between your desire to be excellent and beat others, and your desire to connect and support others. Too often our desire to win overwhelms our desire to connect. Use social view to remind yourself of how valuable people are in your life (see chapter 6). Take a two-pronged approach when you strive for excellence:

1. Seek to compare yourself to earlier versions of yourself, rather than to other people. This will reduce envy. Are you better than you were six months ago? Have you learned something new? Are you finding new ways to enjoy your challenge?

2. Use social view to remember how others feel when they lose and win. During competition, behave with honor, and help people feel good about themselves. Congratulate them when they win; act respectfully when they lose. Then you'll be able to achieve excellence and have excellent relationships.

AFTERWORD

This may be the end of the book, but it isn't the end of your DNA-V journey. Your life is changing in exciting and sometimes challenging ways, but remember, you can always return to this book whenever you face a challenge. Of course, you will need to be skillful to manage changes. Just as a basketball player must continue to practice skills, so must you. Practicing DNA-V skills is a life-long task.

You will need to keep practicing your:

1. **Advisor**, or ability to think well and not let unhelpful thoughts push you around

2. **Noticer**, or ability to pause and take notice of your body, your feelings, and what is going on around you

3. **Discoverer**, or ability to try new behaviors and develop new skills and social connections

4. **Valuer**, or ability to detect what you care about and what gives your life joy, meaning and purpose.

You will need to practice taking different perspectives too:

5. **Self-view,** or the ability to see your DNA-V as constantly changing and growing. You are not fixed. You can grow into the person you want to be

6. **Social-view,** or your ability to connect with others, see different perspectives, and build social connections.

The more you practice flexing your DNA-V muscles, the more you develop flexible strength, and the more you'll be able to live YOUR LIFE YOUR WAY!

Dial into Your DNA-V Strengths

This disk will help you apply flexible strength to a challenge. As you think about a challenging sitaution, answer these questions. What are your evaluations and thoughts (A)? What sensations and feelings do you notice in your body (N)? What might you do in this situation (D)? What kind of person do you want to be in this situation (V)? What aspects of D, N, and A will help you build value?

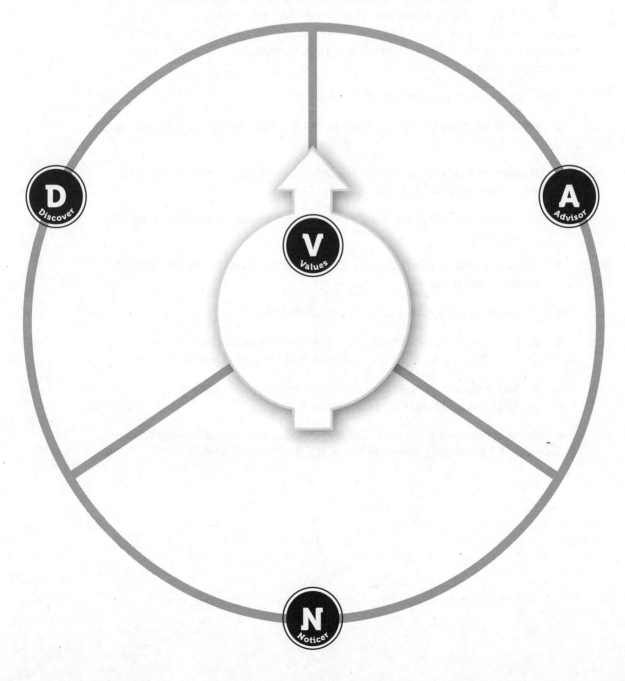

» RESOURCES

Website for Additional Resources

This book is linked to a website that provides resources for teenagers, parents, and educators. Go to http://dnav.international for more resources, including reading, animations, videos, and other items.

Professional Training and Workshops

For a full account of the theoretical and practical applications of DNA-V, see L. Hayes and J. V. Ciarrochi, *The Thriving Adolescent* (Oakland, CA: New Harbinger Publications, 2015). See also J. V. Ciarrochi, L. Hayes, and Ann Bailey, *Get Out of Your Mind and Into Your Life for Teens* (Oakland, CA: New Harbinger Publications, 2012).

Louise Hayes and Joseph Ciarrochi conduct training and speaking engagements around the world for professionals and for young people.

» For more information on Joseph, go to www.josephciarrochi.com

» For more information on Louise Hayes, go to www.louisehayes.com.au

» REFERENCES

This book is based on scientific studies on well-being for young people.

For a full bibliography of the sources we used, please go to:
http://dnav.international

Joseph V. Ciarrochi, PhD, is a professor at the Institute of Positive Psychology and Education at Australian Catholic University, and coauthor of *Get Out of Your Mind and Into Your Life for Teens* and *The Thriving Adolescent*. He has published more than 140 scientific journal articles and many books, including the widely acclaimed *Emotional Intelligence in Everyday Life* and *The Weight Escape*. Ciarrochi has been honored with more than four million dollars in research funding. His work has been discussed on TV and radio, and in magazines and newspaper articles.

Louise L. Hayes, PhD, is an international acceptance and commitment therapy (ACT) trainer and speaker. She is also a clinical psychologist and researcher collaborating on interventions with young people. Hayes has published research trials using ACT for young people, and is coauthor of *Get Out of Your Mind and Into Your Life for Teens* and *The Thriving Adolescent*—the book that introduced DNA-V. She is dedicated to helping young people and their families live well.

Illustrator **Katharine Hall** is based in Wellington, New Zealand. From her wonderful studio in Aotearoa, she tells stories that can translate across language, and specializes in ink work and digital designs for individuals, start-ups, and businesses both big and small.

More  Instant Help Books for Teens

An Imprint of New Harbinger Publications

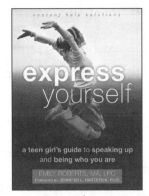

Register your **new harbinger** titles for additional benefits!

When you register your **new harbinger** title—purchased in any format, from any source—you get access to benefits like the following:

- Downloadable accessories like printable worksheets and extra content

- Instructional videos and audio files

- Information about updates, corrections, and new editions

Not every title has accessories, but we're adding new material all the time.

Access free accessories in 3 easy steps:

1. Sign in at NewHarbinger.com (or **register** to create an account).

2. Click on **register a book**. Search for your title and click the **register** button when it appears.

3. Click on the **book cover or title** to go to its details page. Click on **accessories** to view and access files.

That's all there is to it!

If you need help, visit:

NewHarbinger.com/accessories

new harbinger
CELEBRATING
40 YEARS